200 Ways T[Your Expenses: 6 Manuscripts

Learn How To Live Frugal And Start Saving Money

Included Books

Living Frugal And Loving It

Living Frugal And Thriving

Cutting Back And Loving It

Downsizing Your Life And Loving It

Cheapskate Living And Loving It

Habit Stacking For Frugal Living

Table of Contents

Book 2: Living Frugal And Thriving

Chapter 7: Some Helpful Extra Tips

Conclusion

Book 3: Cutting Back And Loving It

Book 4: Downsizing Your Life And Loving It

Book 5: Cheapskate Living And Loving It

Book 6: Habit Stacking For Frugal Living

LIVING FRUGAL

And *Loving It*

40 CREATIVE WAYS TO SAVE MONEY AND LIVE DEBT FREE FOR LIFE

KATHY STANTON

Introduction

I want to thank you for downloading the book, *"Living Frugal and Loving It: 40 Creative Ways To Save Money And Live Debt Free For Life."*

This book contains proven steps and strategies on how you can spend less and save more, by making simple, easy to follow changes in your day-to-day life.

While many people think that living frugally means you have to deny yourself the things you love, this doesn't have to be the case. Instead, be realistic about what you can do, and find small, practical ways to create big changes! In this definitive guide, we've listed 40 tips and tricks that will benefit you on your path to frugal living, ultimately helping you gain the financial freedom you desire.

Thanks again for downloading this book, I hope you enjoy it!

Chapter 1: Looking at the Big Picture

With the cost of living increasing every year, there is no better time than the present to take a look at your day-to-day life, and find places where you could be saving money and reducing waste. Below are some simple tips that will help get you started.

1. **Use less**

   While this may seem like common sense, many of us would be shocked to realize how much we waste daily, in almost every facet of our lives. Most of us could afford to use less in numerous areas including: food, beauty products, gas, clothing, natural resources, and other consumables. Think about enacting small changes like trying to use less toothpaste when you brush, or ensuring that you use only enough laundry detergent to wash the load size you have. For many of us our impulse seems to be more is better, and we don't even try to limit ourselves when we should. Try to be conscious of your consumption and your costs will reduce.

2. **List your goals**

   It can prove very helpful if you jot down a list of your long-term priorities, such as saving for a house, or remodeling a current home. When you have set financial goals you are working toward, it is much easier to remain focused on saving money to achieve that goal. Try to make sure that your savings are only going toward these further out goals, and not being spent on short-tem goals such as vacations. If you have short-term goals you'd like to achieve, try to draw the money from other areas of your budget, such as entertainment or eating out.

3. **Plan ahead**

   While this is easy enough to say, it can often prove much more difficult to implement. If you make it a habit to think far in advance about what is going on in your life, you will ultimately save a significant amount of money. For example, if you know that you will be traveling, make sure to pack a dinner or a lunch. If you find yourself unprepared you'll likely eat your meal at a restaurant (at an increased cost). If you know that you'll be out all day, grab a reusable bottle of water to avoid paying significantly more if you have to purchase it. Is there an important birthday coming up? Grab a gift on sale in advance instead of scrambling the day of for an appropriate present.

4. **Look in advance for significant purchases**

   It is always in your best interest to look in advance, and do your research, before making any decisions on a significant purchase. For big expenditures like appliances or vehicles, keep your eyes peeled for sales, and don't be in a rush. Have a clear idea of what you want, and what a general cost might be both new and used. Often if you have patience, and a strong knowledge of what something is worth, a deal may present itself.

5. **Never buy things full price**

   While this is a rule you can't always stick to, it is one that you should always aim for if at all possible. If you need something take the time to research the standard price and possible sale prices, as well as any discounts or coupons that may apply. Consider also your buying options such as online or in store. Try to buy things like clothing in the off-season when items are likely to be reduced to sell. Keep in mind that many retailers will have a price-match policy, so knowing your stuff will ensure that you can take full advantage of this option.

6. **Re-evaluate your transportation**

   One of the more significant costs that a household can incur is that of owning and operating a vehicle. Between car payments, gas, insurance, and general maintenance, your car can often be a serious financial drain. Why not try riding your bike, walking, or if your city has it, making use of public transit? If you need a car you can always rent one, and you'll probably still save thousands of dollars a year. If saying goodbye to your car is not an option for you, explore the idea of carpooling. Carpooling allows multiple people to share the cost of gas, parking, and other car-related incidentals that can often add up.

7. **Hand make your gifts**

   While not everyone is an artist, with the proliferation of DIY online tutorials, and the social networking site Pinterest, almost anyone can whip up a creative and thoughtful gift. Taking the time to make a gift for someone not only shows a level of care that they will appreciate, it will often end up saving you a significant amount of money.

8. **Consider used first**

   While it can be tempting to own something shiny and new, used is always a good option to explore. When you are looking for a specific item, put out feelers to see if anyone you know, or any of their connections, are selling something similar. Ask around, send out an email, or post your request on a community board (either online or in high traffic areas where you live). You'll be surprised how often what you need it out there, and by reaching out, you are giving someone else a chance to get rid of something they may no longer want, while still getting what you need. If none of your direct contacts have what you are looking for, you can always check online sites such as Craigslist or Freecycle, to see if there are any possible bargains there. A great way to do this is to have a running list of items that you are looking for, so that you are not just focusing on one. Refer back to these sites often to see if there are any new items that catch your eye. If it is not on your list, don't buy it! These sites should be used to make you more frugal, not lead to you buying more stuff.

9. **Focus on increasing your income**

   While online sites such as Craigslist or eBay can be great resources when you are looking to purchase items, they can also bring you extra income. Post items you no longer want that may have value to someone else. You can often make a little money on things you would otherwise just get rid of. Also, try exploring whether you can pick up extra cash by doing freelance or contract work. Websites like oDesk and Elance will put you in contact with clients who need work done on a per job basis, which allows you to fit it into your schedule. Take any extra income you make this way and ensure that you put it directly into savings, so that it doesn't get eaten up but non-essential costs.

Chapter 2: Eating & Entertaining on a Budget

From entertaining at home, to reducing your food bill, there are many ways to limit your costs that don't have to mean sacrificing the things you love. Look no further than your kitchen when you are searching for ways to save.

10. **Eat out less**

    One of the largest, most unnecessary daily expenditures that people make, is eating outside of the home. The average person wastes over $2,000 a year visiting fast-food chains and dining in restaurants. This can be expensive, never mind bad for your health (which can also have long term effects on your spending if you become ill). It is always cheaper to prepare you own food. Try creating a weekly menu and sticking to it. It is important that eating out becomes the exception, and not the rule in your household. If you do have to eat at a restaurant, try a few tips that will make sure your bill doesn't break the bank. Skip the alcohol or soft drinks, and instead ask for water. Water will fill you up and cause you to consume less, while also being free! Perhaps consider splitting a meal with someone, as most places offer ridiculous, unnecessary portions. You'll be looking after your health, and your wallet, and if you feel silly doing it, you've saved enough money to lessen your embarrassment by giving the server a great tip.

11. **Cut coupons and search for vouchers**

    Coupons and vouchers are a valuable tool in a frugal

person's arsenal. Check weekly flyers, clip coupons when you see them, and search online for codes and vouchers. Deals will be offered in almost every area that you spend in, so keep your eyes peeled! Know however, that while coupons and vouchers can save you money, it only works if you purchase things that you normally would. Don't clip coupons for luxury items that you wouldn't usually buy. Coupons should assist you with the necessities, not add another shopping item to your list. necessities

12. **Brown paper bag your lunches**

Absolutely everyone has the ability to plan ahead and pack a lunch, and anyone who uses time constraints as an excuse isn't using their money saving smarts. A packed or prepared lunch will often cost less than $3, and take you only a few minutes to throw together. In comparison, eating out or grabbing something quickly, will more likely fall in the $7 - $20 range. This is one area where people are constantly careless, thoughtlessly cutting into their money saving potential by make hasty eating decisions.

13. **Cook ahead of time**

For many people cooking a week or even a month in advance can be an amazing way to save money. Plan a free day where you can cook food in large batches and then freeze them in dinner-sized potions. While this isn't something that people can do all the time, it can save money if utilized even occasionally. There is a fair amount of planning involved in this, but once completed it will remove the day-to-day meal planning that often poses an issue for overworked and exhausted people. Often when we are tired we revert to eating out or grabbing convenience foods, and having easy, available options at home will at least curb that tendency.

14. **Get a deep freeze**

    Investing in a large freezer can be a great way to save yourself some money down the line. Lots of space will ensure that you can preplan your meals in advance, as well as buy perishable items in bulk. Try stocking up on certain foods when they are on sale, and keep them in the deep freeze until you need them. Reduced cuts of meat, homemade bread, and fresh fruits and vegetables bought when in season, can all be safely stored in the freezer for future use. Knowing that you have a full freezer of available options can also be a comfort to people during times when money isn't quite as plentiful.

15. **Search out affordable recipes**

    There are numerous online sites, as well as specialized cookbooks, that will provide you with affordable, nutritious recipe options. Especially if you are a newbie in the kitchen (but even if you are not), these sites and books can prove invaluable. These sources will often inform you on a variety of topics including the best, most affordable cuts of meat to use in recipes, as well as what is in season (and often priced lower) at certain times of the year. Recipes may also offer a general cost per portion, which can be helpful information for people trying to make better financial choices.

16. **Grow and make your own food**

    Growing your own garden can be an amazing way to cut costs in the kitchen. Think of the vegetables and herbs that you use most, and plant them in the spring, to reap the benefits in the summer. A garden can yield a significant amount of food, and an overabundance of it can always be frozen or canned for later use. Explore also making your own versions of food you can purchase in the store. Make your own bread, try dehydrating fruit, or look up recipes for fresh homemade versions of food you can buy premade, such as hummus or guacamole.

17. **Buy in bulk**

    While many sales and buy-one-get-one-free offers are designed to convince you to buy things you normally wouldn't, there are usually a few items worth grabbing at a reduced price. Be on the lookout for sales and specials on non-perishable items that you frequently need such as canned goods, pasta, and rice. These are items that you know you will eventually use, so if you can find a good deal stock up. Only buy in bulk for these types of necessities or you could end up with items you don't want or need.

18. **Have a concept of the average prices for common goods**

    Being prepared and doing your homework is a major component of staying thrifty when you are grocery shopping. Do a little detective work before you head out and compare the cost of food staples at different stores available to you. See if you can deduce any trends in the items that are usually more affordable at each store. You may end up having multiple grocery stores that each offer something that you want. For example one may be generally the most affordable, while another may have the best prices for meat or produce. Try to organize you grocery shopping to ensure that you are getting what you need from each store. If you don't have a solid concept of what an average price is, you leave yourself susceptible to purchases that may be significantly more than you would have paid elsewhere.

19. **Make your own alcohol**

If you entertain regularly, or if you enjoy a glass of wine or a cold beer, it can often be very cost efficient for you to look into making your own alcohol. While there is some cost for set-up if you are making it out of your own house, it will quickly be absorbed when you realize you are stocking your wine cellar and beer fridge for a fraction of what you would pay in stores. If you like the price point but aren't willing to do all the work, there are many make your own wine and beer facilities that will help you with the process, while still offering a significantly lower cost per bottle.

20. **Entertain your friends at home**

Are you a social butterfly who loves spending quality time with your friends, but doesn't necessarily have the budget for dinner and drinks on the town? Why not trying hosting a night-in at your place, where people can each bring a different snack or potluck dish, and you can organize games or a movie viewing? This may require a little more planning than a trip to a restaurant, but your wallet will reap the benefits. Keep in mind that if you are planning a party where an invitation is required, you can use online services like Evite to take advantage of free, or low-cost options. If you need supplies such as napkins, cups, or plates, stock up when you see them on sale, or hit up your local dollar store. Spending time with your friends doesn't have to mean spending tons of cash.

21. **Drink more water**.

This one seems simple because it is. Water is refreshing and hydrating, and even more importantly to the frugal – it's free! Cut out alcohol, soft drinks, coffee, tea and juices, and you'll find immediately that you have a little extra cash in your pocket.

Chapter 3: Health & Beauty Hacks to Save Money

While keeping ourselves looking and feeling good is important, there are ways that we can ensure that we are still being financially conscious, and watching our consumption. While you don't have to scrimp, here are a few helpful hints on how to save a little cash while still taking care of yourself.

22. **Don't buy name brand over the counter medication**

    For many common medications such as pain relievers or anti-histamines, the ingredients are virtually identical when you compare name brand and generic. Check bulk stores for large bottles of the medications you use, and when there is a choice, opt for the house brand. There is absolutely no difference in how they will work. Also, try searching online for a greater choice of generic brands that may be even more affordable. Often you can score a great deal just by shopping around and checking your options.

23. **Ditch the gym**

    For many people a gym membership is something they underutilize at the best of times, while for others it is a complete waste of money. Regardless of whether you make use of a membership or not, know that there are many other options for keeping fit that you can explore for a fraction of the cost of the gym. Walk, run, cycle, or just get outside! If you'd rather stick close to home, look into the numerous online resources that offer free yoga, fitness, and dance classes (among other options). There are ways to keep fit that don't have to break the bank. Remember though, while we don't advise you shell out a ton of money on the gym, keep in mind that maintaining your physical fitness is an investment you should make. When you focus on preventative care you are ensuring a future not bogged down by poor health and the financial issues that often accompany it.

24. **Good to the last drop**

While many of us like to pretend that we are super conscious about wasting our resources, we often act quite carelessly with things that cost us money. We may casually toss a not quite empty toothpaste because we can't get it from the bottom of the tube, or throw out a moisturizer because it doesn't come out with quite the same quantity as before. In order to be thrifty it is important to ensure that we are using everything to the last drop. We can do this by cutting up tubes and emptying them completely before we throw them away.

Chapter 4: Checking Your Financial Fitness

Being financially in the know can be liberating, and having a solid grasp on where to cut, and where to save, can really help you on your path to financial freedom. Keep a close eye on your funds and make use of the tips below.

25. **Bank smarter**

    Banking smarter means making any number of small changes that will increase the amount of money that you are saving. A great way to get started is by switching your bank account over to a provider who offers no-fee accounts. There is no reason you should be paying maintenance or usage fees, so find someone who will offer you an alternative. Try also to see if you can negotiate credit card or loan interest rates with you bank. It never hurts to ask, and often you will receive! Banking is a competitive business, so if they can't offer you a deal that makes you happy, look elsewhere. Keep in mind though, that one surefire way to save yourself money is by reducing any unnecessary credit you may be paying interest on. Have a credit card if it is absolutely necessary, but keep the balance low, or pay it off monthly to ensure that you aren't wasting dollars that could be going elsewhere.

26. **Have an automatic savings plan**

    A great way to start flexing your frugality muscles is by

transferring money automatically off of your paychecks. Put this money directly into a savings account, and consider it not part of the money you can spend. We tend to try to live to whatever means we have, so often bigger paychecks just means more spending. Remove the extra cash from the equation and see what you can make due with. 20% is a great starting point, but evaluate how that works for you and increase or decrease accordingly. If you don't see the money, chances are you won't miss it. The only stipulation to this rule is if you are carrying significant debt. If this is the case only have a small emergency savings fund, as you want to be allocating money to debt, which is a serious money drain that you should try to remove.

27. **Use a rewards credit card**

While the truly frugal would advocate for no credit, rewards credit cards can be a great option for those who have a solid handle on their spending. Often new cards will offer sign-up bonuses in cash, air miles, or points. If you can take advantage of these responsibly, and not increase your consumption at all, this can be a great benefit. This is essentially extra money that you wouldn't have had otherwise. Using your rewards cards to pay for everything, including bills, will help you amass benefits that you wouldn't with a debit card. This can only work if you spend responsibly though. Running up a credit card to get air miles doesn't work if you are spending hundreds every month in interest.

Chapter 5: Targeting the Technology Cash Drain

We live in a world dominated by technology, and for many of us it is an absolute necessity. Take some time however to consider if there are any technological conveniences you can cut or reduce to save yourself some dollars.

28. **Limit your devices**

    While it can be fun to have all the new gadgets that litter the market, try to really consider what you need technology wise. If your job requires you to write briefs or create complex presentations, then a laptop may be necessary. If however, you end up using your laptop purely to surf the net or check emails, you might consider just having a smart phone that does everything you need at a reduced cost. Many people also have cross over in the devices that they own, owning multiple items that do the same things. One person doesn't need an IPod, IPhone, IPad and Mac computer, but it is very likely that many people possess all of these things. Try to really evaluate your needs and downsize when not necessary.

29. **Cut your cable**

    Gone are the days when cable television connected you to everything that was happening in the world. With the advent of online sites where you can view virtually anything you want, and the arrival of very low cost subscription packages, cable is no longer a necessity for many households. Save some cash by downsizing or removing an expensive package, and pick and choose what you want from affordable online options. Often cable leads to endless channel surfing, and killing time watching things you aren't really interested in. A positive side effect of ditching it is that you may only end up watching television for specific programs, leading to less time wasted on the couch.

30.   Negotiate with your providers

Many companies that provide services like phone and internet service, can afford to be more flexible than they would have you believe. Just because they present you with a price, doesn't mean that is the final offer. Don't be afraid to call customer service and let them know that you are exploring other options. Check in with them every few months and see what new deals they are offering to new clients. Once they've already secured your business they certainly won't be calling you to reduce your bill, but if they can offer to new people, they should be able to offer it to you. It never hurts to ask, and often you can secure some great deals.

Chapter 6: Don't be House Poor

Your home is your palace, and for many of us (especially those trying to cut back on costs) it is where we spend the majority of our time. Ensure that your home isn't a drain on your finances by following the tips below.

31. **Get the house you NEED, not the house you WANT**

    In the competitive housing market banks often try to offer incredibly low interest rates and high mortgage approvals to entice buyers. Just because you are approved for a $500,000 mortgage, doesn't mean you have to take it. Think seriously about what type of house possesses all of the things you need, without veering too far into what you want on top of that. You may be able to find a house for $200,000 that fits all of your criteria, so don't be tempted by the more expensive house. While it may be nicer, if the other house fits your conditions, there is no logical reason to pay more. Keep in mind that you may think you can afford a larger mortgage, but when you factor in utilities, property taxes, upkeep, and unexpected incidentals that will arise, you may be in for more than you bargained for.

32. **Ensure the efficiency of your home**

    Your home can often be one of the major money drains in your life. While some things are beyond your control, there are a few things you can do to ensure that your house isn't siphoning money directly from your savings. First, ensure that it is properly insulated. This can include checking for any places that heat might escape from, and windows are often a key culprit. Make sure that windows are not a heat drain, and replace anything that threatens to hike up your bills. If you can't afford to replace windows you can cover them with plastic in the cooler months to keep warm air from escaping and cooler air getting in. Also, ensure that you are using appliances and electricity wisely. Turn off lights when you leave a room, and try not to use water for laundry or dishwashing during peak hours. Finally, try not to fiddle too much with your thermostat. Even moving it by a few degrees can seriously affect your utility bills. Throw on a sweater or invest in a pair of slippers, and your bank account will thank you.

33. **Make your own cleaning products**

While supermarket cleaning products can often cost a premium, a quick look in your cupboards may offer you a multitude of ingredients that can also do the trick, at a fraction of the price. Try using a teaspoon of bicarbonate of soda on a damp cloth to mimic a cream cleanser. White vinegar is also an amazing all-purpose ingredient whether you are washing your windows or cleaning your floors. There is absolutely no reason to pay high prices for brand-name items when you can do a quick search on the internet that will reveal numerous cleaning product recipes that will save you money, and keep your house spotless.

34. **Master the art of DIY**

While there are some things, like plumbing and electrical, which should be left to professionals, there are a lot of do-it-yourself tricks that you can employ to save yourself some money. Online tutorials in how to do small repairs around your home make undertaking household projects that much easier. You can also visit your larger hardware stores for information on projects like tiling and painting. When you fix something yourself, you not only gain a serious sense of accomplishment, you also save money!

Chapter 7: Looking Good For Less

While it can be fun to have new clothes, this is a major area of expenditure for a lot of people, and one of the most obvious places that you can make changes for the better. Consider these tips below before buying new, or tossing the old.

35.   Wash clothes less

While some people wear clothes once and then throw them in the wash, this isn't necessarily the best way to maintain the colour and quality of your items. Unless you have a job which involves your clothes getting extremely dirty, or you hit the gym and sweat profusely, most clothes can be worn more than once before tossing them in the wash. Use the smell test to deduce whether they are actually dirty or not. You'll know right away if they can stick around for another wear, or if it is time to put them in the hamper. This can save you money on washing, but it will also serve to extend the life of your clothing.

36.   Hang-dry clothes

While dryers are fast, they aren't always the best option if you are looking to curb energy usage and prolong the life of your clothing. Especially if you are doing smaller loads, take a few minutes to hang them up. If the sun is shining they'll be dry before you know it, but even drying on racks inside can be better for your items and save your electricity bills. Air-drying means that nothing is being shrunk or damaged, and this can save you even more money in the long run when you don't have to buy new clothes.

37. Shop at consignment boutiques

Clothing shopping is another area where you can opt to buy used. Visit consignment shops where you can often find high-quality items at a seriously reduced price. In fact, many items will be barely used, and if you have patience you should be able to land yourself a few great pieces. When shopping vintage you can also raid your parents' or grandparents' old closets for pieces from previous decades. You can hit on some really beautiful items that may be the height of fashion this way. Don't let snobbery or distaste for second-hand, stop you from finding amazing bargains.

38.   Spend money on quality

While it often seems counterintuitive when you are trying to be frugal, it is often wise to pay more money for clothing than less. Often cheaper items are low quality and won't be able to hold out long enough for you to refresh them or prolong their life. High quality items may come with a higher price tag, but try to think of them as investments. Buy staples that you can wear for years, instead of disposable clothing that won't last a season. Evaluate the quality of clothing by checking the stitching for loose threads, and ensure that any patterns match up. Try also bunching the material in your hand for a few seconds and then watch if it returns to its natural shape. Make smart fashion choices and you should have high-quality items for more than long enough to justify the cost.

39.   Take care of your clothes

While day-to-day wear and tear is unavoidable, you can often prolong the life of your clothing with a few simple steps. Instead of throwing away fuzzy sweaters use a razor blade to remove pilling and refresh the wool. Try also dying faded jeans, or digging out the sewing machine to repair any clothing with missing buttons or small holes. If you are bored of what is in your closet, try to get creative by bringing new life to old items. Head to markets or sewing shops and find artistic supplies to jazz up tired old apparel. Check fashion magazines and internet images for inspiration, and make it your own!

40.   Host a clothing swap

A clothing swap can be a great way to get rid of items you no longer want, while acquiring new ones at no cost! Ask your girlfriends to go through their closets and bring items they want to get rid of. Have them bring everything to a get-together where everyone gets to sort through and pick out the items they like. Throw in some appetizers and wine and you've got a party! This idea can also be extended to include children's clothing, if you have a group of mothers with kids of differing ages.

Conclusion

Thank you again for downloading this book!

I hope this book was able to help inspire you to immediately start looking at the ways in which you can limit consumption, and save money in your daily life.

The next step is to cultivate a conscious awareness of the ways in which you can make use of the tips and tricks in this book, ensuring yourself the financial freedom and security you desire.

Thank you and good luck!

LIVING FRUGAL AND THRIVING

40 Different Ways To Develop A Frugal Mindset, Simplify Your Life And Enjoy Life On A Budget

KATHY STANTON

Introduction

I want to thank you for downloading the book, Living Frugal And Thriving: 40 DIY Frugal Living Hacks That Will Help You Spend Less And Save More!

In this book you are going to learn how to begin living a frugal lifestyle so that you can save more money and still have everything that you need. You will learn everything from how to save money on your grocery bill to DIY décor for your house. I will also share with ways to save money while having fun and doing the things you love!

In addition, I'll provide you with money saving tips on ways to cut down on your electric bill and other monthly utilities. By the time you finish this book you'll be equipped with everything you'll need to know in order to begin living a frugal lifestyle and still be able to enjoy your life. Let's get started!

Thanks again for downloading this book, I hope you enjoy it!

Chapter 1

How to Eat on a Budget

Most of us know what it is like to struggle each week. We get our check, pay our bills and have no idea how we will make it until the following week. One of the biggest bills that we have to deal with on a regular basis is our grocery bill. This is the one bill that no matter what we do, we still have to buy groceries. So I want to go over some great tips that will help you save as much as possible on your grocery bill.

I hope that at this point you are already shopping the sales, using coupons and cutting back on your snacks. This will always help to cut back on your grocery bill. However, those are just the basics. I want to give you some more tips and strategies that you can use to cut your grocery bill.

1. The first tip I want to give you is that you should only do your major grocery shopping once per month. At first this will be a little bit difficult especially if you have kids. You will have to plan out each of the meals you will be having, as well as snacks. You have to take into consideration that fresh fruits and vegetables only last a few weeks in the fridge and that by the end of the month you will be eating canned fruits and vegetables. It may also be difficult because I have found that when you purchase a large amount of food at one time, people tend to forget that it has to last a month and they eat a lot more than they should. You will have to keep reminding everyone in your family that this food is for

the month and make it clear that if it is all eaten they will have nothing left before you go shopping again.

It may take a few months of this for your family to really get used to the fact that you will only be shopping once a month, but it will happen. When it comes to using milk to cook with, try to find some soy milk that can be kept in the cabinet. This ensures that even if someone drinks that last bit of milk in the fridge you don't have to go out and spend $5 on a new gallon. You can find this soy milk at one dollar stores and I advise you to purchase a few just in case you need to cook with them. These are also great to use in cereal.

2. Learn how to cook once and eat two or three times. One example of this is when you make chicken and dumplings. You will first cut up your chicken and boil it for the dumplings. Use only the white meat for the dumplings. Once the dark meat has cooled, you can put it in the crock pot with some barbeque sauce and have barbequed chicken sandwiches. Another idea is that you can make a roasted chicken, using the leftover meat make barbequed chicken sandwiches and use the bones and skin to make a broth for chicken noodle soup. Be creative and see how far you can stretch a meal.

3. Stop wasting. This goes a long with the previous tip, but you should go further than this. So many times we throw that barbeque sauce bottle in the trash before adding water and getting the extra sauce out. This goes for everything you use from dish soap to laundry detergent to all of your condiments. You also need to make sure that all of the lids are placed tightly back onto a container when it is opened. Often times children especially will just place the cap back on a

container and the item will spoil after it sets for a little while. If you really want to stop wasting you need to consider eating leftovers as well. There is no reason why you cannot take your leftover chicken noodle soup to work with you for lunch instead of going out and spending $7 on an unhealthy fast food meal.

4. Speaking of unhealthy, you are actually going to save more money if you consider your health. When you pick up an item at the store you need to ask yourself how it is going to benefit your body? If you want to really save money you need to purchase items that are going to fill you up and keep you full for a long time. You also want to purchase items that are going to give your body the nutrients that it needs and not just something that is cheap.

5. Avoid packaged processed foods. If you want to eat Salisbury steaks, that is fine, learn how to make them from scratch. They will be cheaper, more filling and healthier than if you purchased the prepackaged option. Soda is another item you should consider removing from your diet. If you just can't stand the thought of drinking plain water, go for some koolaid mix where you will control the amount of sugar in it or lemonade. Even flavored water is a great option. You will save a ton on sugary soda and you will find that you feel better after you stop drinking it as well!

6. Learn how to bake. Many people find that they are wasting a lot of money on unhealthy snacks. One way you can avoid this is to learn how to bake. Making a cake once a week should last a family of four the entire week, if it is used as a small snack or small desert. If you are not an avid baker but want to have a cake like the pros make, simply follow the directions on a cake mix box but ad 1 extra egg, use butter instead of oil and milk instead of water. You will never miss those pre ordered cakes again.

There are many ways that you can cut back on your grocery bill but you will have to have an open mind and you will have to be creative. You may have to learn how to cook new recipes that you have never tried before and you may have to be open to trying new foods. No matter what it is that you do in order to cut your food budget, it is imperative that you take the time to create a meal plan. Without a plan you have no direction and will always end up spending much more than you really want to.

Chapter 2

Retail, I Think Not!

I remember the days when I had no problem paying retail for all of the items that I purchased. It never crossed my mind that I would be able to save at least 50 percent off of retail and still get the items I wanted and needed.

1. Sales are a huge deal. One of my most recent joys was that I found out most of my local stores run huge sales that I didn't even know about. I am talking 70 to 90 percent off sales. They rotate from home décor to kitchen essentials, appliances and so on. The way I found this was that I was looking for coupon groups for different stores on Facebook and on top of the coupon matchups they began posting these different sales they were finding. I was recently able to get a $25 pot for $2.50. Of course I grabbed a few because I never want to have to go pay $25 dollars for that pot. I was also able to get a ton of home décor for 70 percent off as well as 18 count packs of wash cloths for .40 cents each. You never have to pay full price and if you want to really start saving money and living frugally you need to start watching for these types of sales.

2. Another way to ensure that you do not pay retail is to watch for items that are being discontinued. This is where a lot of these Facebook groups come in handy because a store is not going to advertise that an item is being discontinued. One recent item I was able to

purchase was old spice 2 in one hair and body wash. These are normally $4 but since they were being discontinued I was able to get them for .40 cents each. I have also seen diaper packaging that has been discontinued and a pack of diapers that would normally sell for $25 only costs $3. Match this up with a coupon and you wouldn't have to buy diapers for a very long time!

3. End of season sales are the next way to ensure you do not pay retail. We recently did all of our shopping for next years winter clothes. Now, I should note that right now while I am writing this book it is the beginning of May. I paid no more than $1 per each piece of clothing and the majority of the pieces retailed for over $25 dollars! I also just finished shopping for next years Easter baskets (all but the candy) I was able to purchase $123 worth of Easter items and I paid $12. This is only because I hit the sale after the holiday. It is just like an end of season sale but a few weeks after each holiday all of the items for that holiday go on sale for up to 90 percent off. You can purchase any item you need this way, a swimming pool, a lawn mower, absolutely anything.

4. Stock up when the price is right. You should be using coupons with your sales. I am not going to go over how to use coupons, how important they are if you really want to save money, and all the other information that goes along with couponing. However, what I will tell you is that when your coupon matches a sale and you find a stock up price, get as many as you can. One example of this is recently I was able to purchase Nivea body wash which sells for $2.50 a bottle for only .12 cents per bottle. Needless to say I have 50 of them. I will not need to purchase body wash again until this sale comes around next time and will not pay $2.50 per bottle ever again. This goes for food items as well as any other item that you need.

5. Keep track of the prices you are willing to pay. Just because something is on sale does not mean that it is a good deal. You need to decide what price you are willing to pay. For example, I will not pay more than .25 cents per roll of toilet paper, more than $3 for a bottle of All laundry detergent, or more than $4 for quality shampoo and conditioner. I also know that I do not have to pay more than .25 cents per pound of Pedigree dog food. This allows me to know when I will stock up and when a good deal should be taken advantage of. If you go into a store without knowing the price you are willing to pay for the items you purchase on a regular basis, you are going to spend far too much money.

When I say never pay retail I do mean never. By setting the price you are willing to pay for the items you purchase you are the one that is in charge of your budget. You don't have to worry when prices go up because you know that you have enough of any specific item to last until the next sale. I should note that in the beginning it may seem like you are spending a little more than you would like. For example if you can purchase pasta for .10 cents a box and you get 50 of them, you may spend a bit more on pasta than you normally would that week but you need to look at how much you will save in future weeks.

Chapter 3

Decorating Your Home on a Budget

Of course you can save money decorating your home by using some of the previous tips, such as watching sales, but I think it is important to spend a little bit of time focusing on this topic. Many people think that when they are trying to live frugally they think that the lifestyle has to be reflected in the way their home looks as well, but that is not true. You can have a beautiful home while still living frugally.

1. Thrift stores are a great place to get large pieces of furniture. I was recently able to purchase a couch that is just like new for $20. I was also able to get some beautiful pictures, flowers and other décor. By the time I left the thrift store I had spent $40, bought new furniture and redecorated my entire living room. Thrift stores should be one of the first places you look when you need to make a large furniture purchase. The only down side is that most likely they do not deliver so you will have to have a way to haul the purchases back to your home.

2. If you find some furniture that has a really good structure to it but you don't like the pattern, use slip covers to ensure all of your furniture matches. Slipcovers can be purchased fairly cheap and if you are placing them on furniture you purchased from a thrift store, you will still save a ton compared to purchasing new items. Here is an example, the couch I purchased

for $20 has a floral pattern. I don't like floral patterns so I purchased a slip cover for $25. My total spent on this piece was $45 which is obviously much less than what I would have paid for a brand new couch.

3. Don't feel like you have to have every space in your home filled. If you are one of those people who just cannot stand to have empty wall space or an empty space in the room, this may be a little difficult for you. Personally I hate clutter and would rather have a lot of space instead of items. Focus on making your home look and feel comfortable and not on collecting as many items as you possibly can. If your home feels crowded or you are looking around right now realizing you have no empty space, you may want to consider selling some of the items you already have.

4. If you really want to update the look of a room, ask your local store if they have any custom paint color returns. You can usually get these at a deep discount and update any room in your home with them! You can also use these colors to add a little life to old wooden furniture that you purchase for next to nothing at thrift stores. You may end up finding colors that you really fall in love with. Before spending a ton of money on paint, make sure you check out the returns first.

5. Don't get too caught up in changing your décor with the season. Personally my favorite colors are fall colors. My entire house is decorated with these colors. Even though we are getting ready for summer, I do not plan to change things out. Purchase items you love and instead of worrying about keeping up with everyone else, you will be able to come home knowing that you love the way it looks.

There are always low cost ways to decorate your home. You can make curtains out of fabric you find at resale shops, you can create your own artwork or just keep an eye out for items that truly speak to you. All you need to worry about is making sure that your home is a space where you can relax and where you can enjoy those you love.

Chapter 4

Electric Bills Sucking You Dry?

There are also many things that we can do on a daily basis to ensure that we are saving all of the money possible. I want to go over a few tips that you can use to save you money on your utilities. Of course we all know that we should turn our lights off after we leave a room and unplug appliances that are not in use, but I want to give you some more in depth tips in this chapter in case the basics are not cutting your electric bill enough.

1. Currently it is 83 degrees outside and if I were not living a life of saving money I would have my air conditioner set on about 70. Right now it is 74 degrees in my house and I have to say even with no air conditioner I am comfortable. The way that I keep my electric bill as low as possible is to open my windows at night allowing fresh cool air into my home. As soon as I wake up in the morning, my windows get shut, trapping that cool air inside. Now I am not going to lie, with kids running in and out all day long my house does not stay as cool as I would like it to be, but I am not sweating and I am not going to die. Remind yourself that people lived for years without air conditioning and it is not going to kill you to go without. If you cannot handle not using the AC at all this summer, try setting it to about 78 degrees or higher. You will be amazed at how low you can get your electric bill by just reducing the amount of time you use the air conditioning. Of course the same goes for your heater in the winter.

2. Get your laundry done and keep it that way. Many people will allow their laundry to pile up and then do it once per week. This means that your dryer is running nonstop for most of the weekend. Did you know that it is actually cheaper to run the washer and dryer once per day everyday of the week? In many cases electric companies charge less for electricity used during the evening than they do for electricity used during the day, so if you wash one load of laundry each evening you will be paying less per load than if you wash it on the weekends. It is also cooler in the evening, so if you are running your dryer you will not heat your house up as much causing your air conditioner to kick on in the summer.

3. While we are on the subject of laundry, make sure you are washing it in cold water only. Of course you can use hot water for those extremely soiled piece of clothing such as work clothes, but for everyday wear, cold water will work just fine. You should also consider not washing your clothing as often. You know that dress you wore to brunch Sunday morning for 2 hours, instead of throwing it in the laundry pile, hang it back up after you wash it. This is not to say that you should allow your clothing to become disgusting or smelly, but use your best judgement on what really needs washed and what can be worn one more time.

4. Cover your windows with thick curtains. Of course we all love to have natural light in our homes, but in the summer leaving our windows uncovered only causes our homes to heat up faster. If you want to have some natural light, open the curtains that are not getting direct sunlight in the summer and the ones that are getting direct sunlight in the winter. You can use the suns heat in the winter to help heat your home and lower your heating bill.

5. Unplug your cell phone chargers, laptop charges as well as any other electrical item when it is not in use.

Chargers will use electricity if they are charging an item or not and all electrical items will use a little bit of electricity even if they are not turned on. One easy way to make sure you do not have to go around unplugging all the time is to use power surge protectors. When the items are not in use just turn the strip to the off position and it will ensure that no electricity is being used.

Electricity is one of our biggest bills that we have to pay, but it does not have to be that way. Following the tips that I have given you in this chapter will ensure that you are never paying too much for electricity and you are putting as much money as possible back into your pocket. One thing you should be warned of is that you should not allow yourself to feel that just because you have done well on your electricity use all month that you can splurge at the end of the month and turn your air conditioner down. This will cause all of your work to be in vain and you will lose your motivation for saving on electricity very quickly.

Chapter 5

Let's Have Some Fun!

Being frugal does not mean that you are not going to be able to have any fun. Yes you are going to have to spend some extra time cooking your meals at home and working on DIY projects, but you don't have to live a life without any fun just because you want to be frugal. There are plenty of ways to enjoy life and live frugal at the same time.

1. One of the things my family loves to do is swim. We tend to do this on a daily basis when the weather allows, but we are not willing to pay $3 per person per day to swim at the pool. Instead we take off down to the river and spend a few hours splashing around. There are fewer people there and if too many people show up all we have to do is move up stream just a bit. There is always enough room for us at the river. You can also go to the beach or a lake depending on what is in your area. Make sure if you are going to be there for very long you pack some extra food so the kids are not screaming to grab fast food on the way home.

2. Speaking of packing some extra food, picnics are a great way to spend time with your family and not spend any extra money. One thing my kids love to do in the summer is make a picnic lunch and just go out in the yard and eat it. You don't have to go very far, just going outside to eat is a ton of fun for kids. You can also have a night where you cook hotdogs and s'mores over a fire.

This is a great way to relax and spend some time getting some fresh air.

3. Camping was always something that we loved to do when we were kids and still love to do to this day. Pack up the family and spend a few days camping out in the woods. Find an area that does not charge a fee and is close to a river. Have the kids fish for their dinner and save even more. (Always make sure you bring some back up food just in case they don't catch anything.)

4. Take up a hobby that is both fun and saves you money. One thing that myself and my children love to do is clip coupons. This is my hobby, but it is also a way that we can spend time together as a family. You can also go for walks, get exercise while you spend time with your family, get healthy and enjoy nature all at the same time.

5. Get your family involved in some DIY projects. Kids love to help plant a garden and care for it. They love to plant flowers and care for them as well. Get them involved in any project that you are working on and it will not only be fun for them, but it will be a great memory that lasts a lifetime. I guarantee it will mean more to them than the time you took them to an amusement park and wasted $300.

Just because you are living a frugal lifestyle does not mean that you have to be boring. Some of the most interesting people I know live a frugal lifestyle. They are always doing something, working on some project or having fun with their families. They are actually happier than those I know who do not live a frugal lifestyle.

Chapter 6

Everything Else

Being frugal should be incorporated into every area of your life, not just in your bills. One example of this is that I told you about the end of season sales, but what happens if you need a new skirt and you cannot find any on sale? This is when you need the knowledge to fall back on that you will find in this chapter. In this example, you would want to go to a thrift store and try to find a nice skirt before you ever considered paying full price for one. So in order to make sure that we cover everything we can in this book, I want to give you some tips about how to live frugally in all the areas of your life.

1. It seems like almost everyone is downsizing their homes right now and that is a great way to save a ton of money. It does not matter if you are a homeowner or if you are renting your home, if you can live in a smaller home you really should consider downsizing and saving the difference.

2. Buy used and save the difference. This applies to everything. If you cannot get an item on sale for almost free, make sure you check to see if you can buy it used. This applies to your car as well. Even when you are buying used, see if you can get a lower price, this usually works if you are paying cash.

3. While we are on the subject of paying cash, make sure that you are paying cash for all of your purchases. This means that when you go shopping you only take cash, leave the debit and credit cards at home. If you only

have so much money with you, you are less likely to splurge on items you do not actually need.

4. If something breaks, first ask yourself if you really need it. If you do not, then do not replace it. If you do need the item and you do not have enough cash to purchase it, see if you can find a way around purchasing an item. For example, if your lawnmower breaks, of course you want to see if you can get it fixed but if not can you borrow a friends lawnmower once a week until you can afford to buy a new one?

5. Learn how to tell your kids no. This was a huge one for me but the fact is that your kids do not need a toy every time you go to the store. They do not need a candy bar or a soda either. They have toys at home and can wait to eat and drink. Save the gifts for when they are really deserved. If they want items in between holidays or birthdays, let them earn their own money and pay for the items themselves.

Chapter 7

Some Helpful Extra Tips

Of course I have tips for you to live frugally that don't actually fall into any category so I have saved them for this chapter. Some of these are probably the most important tips that you will find in this book.

1. Be content with what you have. I have to say this is the number one tip that you can follow. Don't compare what you have to what everyone else has. Don't allow yourself to simply want something because it is the newest big thing or because all of your friends have it. Think about this. Currently I have an Android smart phone, it cost me $20 and although everyone I know has the latest model iPhone, that does not matter to me. I am able to text, get online and make phone calls. My phone fits my needs and I am content with it.

2. Companies are always giving out free samples. Most of the time all you have to do is sign up for them and you will get a full size product in the mail along with several great coupons that are not available to everyone else. I take five minutes each day and sign up for a few freebies that I really want. This means that every single day I am getting free items in the mail along with money saving coupons for the product should I decide to purchase it.

3. Have a no spend month. If you are using coupons and stocking up on items when you can get them at rock bottom prices this should be very simple to do. Once a year or even twice a year choose to not spend any money for the entire month. Use the food you have in your pantry as well as the rest of the supplies you have stocked up on. Put all of that money in your savings account and once the month is over start following those sales again.

4. Have your children choose one activity to be a part of and limit it to that. There is no reason that children should be involved in every activity available and be busier than adults. If the kids absolutely must be part of other activities, explain to them that these activities cost money and they will have to earn the money for themselves.

5. Exercise is important to us all and if you want to be frugal you do not want to be wasting your money on a gym membership. Instead, you should find ways to exercise that do not cost any money. If you are just starting to exercise, consider looking up beginner videos on YouTube. This is a great resource for those who are more advanced as well. You can also take your dog for a run or just walk around the park for a little while each day.

6. Stop smoking and drinking. This may seem a little bit difficult but you need to consider how much you are paying for these items and what they are doing to your health. Health is a part of being frugal and if you want to save as much money as possible, you need to consider your health bills. Think about the amount of money you will save not only on current doctor bills, but what you will save in the future.

7. Run your errands in batches. Instead of going to pay bills one day and then going grocery shopping one day and then going to get household supplies another day,

designate one day to running all the errands. You should also plan your trip so that you are not having to drive in circles. Plan out your trip so that you are able to go to each place you need using as little gas as possible.

8. Take care of what you have. You have worked hard for the money that you spent on your items, the least you can do is take care of what you already have. By taking care of what you already have, you will find that it lasts longer and you have to replace them less often.

9. Christmas, birthdays and other holidays are expensive. Create a gifting box in your closet out of a storage container. When you find great items on sale place them in the container. When you need an item to give as a gift you don't have to worry about paying full price, just go to your closet and grab the appropriate gifts.

Living a frugal life is amazing. You can have everything you need and not have to worry about not having enough money. It does take a little bit of work and you should make changes over time, but by living a frugal life you will be able to have the life you always dreamed of.

Conclusion

Thank you again for downloading this book!

I hope this book was able to help you to learn how to live a frugal lifestyle and save money.

The next step is to choose some tips and put them into action.

Finally, if you enjoyed this book, then I'd like to ask you for a favor, would you be kind enough to leave a review for this book on Amazon? It'd be greatly appreciated!

Thank you and good luck!

CUTTING BACK AND LOVING IT

50 Creative Ways To Simplify Your Space, Declutter Your Life And Achieve The Life You Desire

KATHY STANTON

Introduction

I want to thank you for downloading the book, *Cutting Back and Loving It: 50 Creative Ways to Simplify Your Space, Declutter Your Life and Achieve the Life You Desire.*

This book contains proven steps and strategies on how to minimize your "stuff" in order to live a clutter-free and enjoyable life. We have all done it. Looking around our home or office, we see the stuff that we wish we could hide. We have visions of a showroom home that is clean and tidy. However, that doesn't follow through into our lives.

Our lives are full of clutter and it can be a huge eyesore to both you and those who visit you. Why do you put up with it? If you're ready for a change, then try some of the creative ways that I will talk about in this book to make your space seem uncluttered and simple. You can have a room that mirrors a showroom with just a few simple changes to your life.

Thanks again for downloading this book, I hope you enjoy it!

Chapter 1- Clutter vs. Necessity

Let's get real here. In a world where quantity definitely overrides quality, people obtain more and more stuff that just ends up piling up. You might find a few good things in your piles, but for the most part, you can probably live without most of the items sitting in front of you at this very moment. All of that stuff that you felt you needed to have is unused and wasted money. Have you ever thought about how you can maintain a simple life and not have so much stuff?

You are not the only one who faces this struggle. With many like you, you have a support system that can help you get past the clutter stage and into the open-feeling stage. It takes time, and it takes patience, but if you are determined to weed out your unwanted and unnecessary belongings, you will find that your home or office will feel more open and free.

However, there is one battle that you have to overcome. What do you own that would be considered clutter and what would be considered necessity? By asking yourself whether or not you really use or need a certain object will help you begin to shed yourself of all the items that just aren't a part of your life. Understanding that they are just things will also help you in the battle to part with items that you might like but don't need.

Take a look around the room that you are sitting in right now. You can probably spot at least a half dozen items that you can easily give away and never miss. Why do you still have them? What is the point in keeping them? Some people tell themselves that they will eventually use them, but eventually doesn't always come. If you are in that mindset, then just save yourself the trouble of planning on using it and get rid of it! This will take care of one piece of clutter in your life!

Once you can differentiate clutter from necessity, you can begin the process of uncluttering your home and making it possible to feel as though you have space to move about. This can be a liberating for you. No one realizes just how much getting rid of unnecessary stuff can really feel! Also, when you have less, it becomes easier to maintain your home, and it also gives you the time and ability to spend time with others. It's a winning situation all around, so why not go for it?

If you feel doubts about parting with items in your life, think about others who could really use what you don't use. By giving your possessions away, you're not only simplifying your life, but you are helping those who need what you have. If you don't use it, and you will never look at it again, then don't be selfish and keep it. You're not only hurting yourself, but you are also hurting someone who can use what you are keeping to yourself.

So, if you're ready to make the change and want to know how you can make these changes, keep on reading! I will provide you with creative ways to declutter your home and simplify your life!

Chapter 2- Tips to Decluttering and Simplifying Your Living Space

Your main living space is what your friends, family and any other visitor that comes around will notice first. Sadly enough, people will judge you by what your home looks like. Seeing that your main living space feels cluttered might give them the wrong impression of you as a person. So, let's focus on how to declutter your living space and making it feel more open and inviting to your visitors.

Picture in your mind what you would like your living space to look like. What can you do to make sure that it look like it does in your mind? Try putting together a list of what will need to be done in order to achieve the picture that you have in your mind.

Getting Rid of the Junk

One of the most time-consuming but most necessary elements of simplifying and decluttering is getting rid of unnecessary items in your home. Deciding on what to get rid of and what to keep can take a lot of time and energy. This can be especially true if you're a person who may place sentimental value in objects. However, we must learn to separate that item from the memory and part with items that are no longer needed or used.

After you have parted with your junk, then you can effectively begin organizing and simplifying your home with what you have left.

Downsizing Furniture

Large furniture can easily take up space and make your home look small and cluttered. Try finding pieces that suit your home and your room sizes. This will allow your room to feel larger and more open. If you live alone, there really is no reason for you to have a full living room set when a chair or a small loveseat would suit you perfectly. Think about the implications your furniture might have on the feel of your home and consider downsizing in order to make your space feel larger.

Arrange Your Furniture in an Inviting Way

If you have too much furniture or not enough space, try rearranging your furniture so that it helps your room feel more inviting and more open. A lot of furniture can be used as room dividers and shelves can be set up behind sofas to create a homey look. Take the furniture you currently have and try arranging it in different ways that make your room feel simple and inviting. It might take a couple of tries, but once you find the arrangement you like, then you will have a living room that will be suitable for guests.

Keep the Décor Simple

One of the most crucial ways to simplify your home is to cut back on your decorations. I will cover this a bit more later on, but having to many decorations will make a room feel full and cluttered, even if the room is large and there is nothing else to make it feel cluttered. Try limiting what you have on your walls, mantle and shelves. Keeping it simple will help it become much more roomy and inviting.

Tone Down the Colors

Bold and dark colors can easily make your room look dark or overwhelming. Try using earthy and light colors. This tip works for both your decorations and for your furniture. The lighter it looks, the more open and airy your room will feel. If you don't like extremely light colors, try medium tones that won't overpower the room and make it feel small. Try looking in decorating magazines and find rooms that appeal to you and try to imitate their decorating style in your own home.

Make Sure it Has Enough Lighting

Sometimes, the rooms in your home will not receive a whole lot of natural lighting. This can make the room feel dark and dreary, even if you have light colored décor. If you have a room like this in your home, try using lamps and other forms of lighting to make the room feel brighter and happier. You can buy many different types of lamps that can light your room and give you the feel that you wish to achieve. Even a dim room can feel cozy if it is lit in the right way.

Have Enough Open Floor Space

If you cannot walk through a room, then you know that you have a problem with clutter. Floor space is important in making your home feel open and simple. If you find that you have too much furniture, then it might be time to consider getting rid of some of it and making your room feel larger. No one wants to dodge furniture with every step in order to make it through that room, and it could lead to accidents in the middle of the night.

Starting my decluttering and organizing your living space can help you to get a feel for what you would like the rest of your home to look like. This might be the largest part of your project, but once your main room feels open and simple, you will get the motivation to continue to work through the rest of your home. Simple doesn't always mean that you go minimalist, it just means that you are making your home feel less cluttered and more inviting. Cutting back on what you have in your living area, whether it be dark colors or too much furniture, can lead to your entire home feeling simpler.

Chapter 3- Tips for Decluttering and Simplifying Your Personal Space

When looking at your personal space, such as your bathroom or bedroom, it might feel like there is a lot of stuff in a small space. Most of the items in the bathroom are more than likely used on a regular basis, so getting rid of them is simply not an option. However, it looks like the cosmetic section at the store blew up in there. There are ways to unclutter these spaces while not getting rid of the items that you don't want to sacrifice.

Decluttering and simplifying doesn't necessarily mean getting rid of everything you own. It also has a lot to do with organization and where items are kept. By rearranging your spaces, you can quite possibly declutter and simplify without having to donate half of your life to the thrift store. Let's take a look at some ways that you can declutter and organize your living space in order to achieve a happier atmosphere.

Bathroom Organization Tools

Every bathroom that I have ever been in has had extremely limited counter space. With so much that I need in my personal beauty routine, how do I deal with not having a counter to spread out on? After careful thought, I decided that I would use other resources in my bathroom that can help me to stay organized and make my bathroom look tidy.

I began by using the wall space. For my styling tools, such as my straightener and blow dryer, I installed hooks on the wall in which I could hang them from their cords when they are not in use. Even if you have tools with retractable cords, you can use something to attach the tool to the hook, such as a piece of strong string.

After I made good use of my wall space, I cleared up my cluttered counters by using small shelves on the walls in which I could store lotions and hair supplies. These helped get them up and off the counter when not in use. All of the other tools I was able to purchase a small set of plastic drawers that I could toss them in and get them out of the way.

Creating Space in Your Closet

Closet space is often the most limited space in your home, and you will more than likely store more stuff in there than in the rest of your home. Before you try to create space, try to get rid of some of the items that make it cluttered. If you were to dig to the back of your closet, you would probably find items that you forgot you even had. Get rid of them and that opens up space right there. After you have gotten rid of what you can, then try using shelving and hooks to store what is being kept. Getting some of the items off the floor and off of the hangers can help you to create more space.

Making the Most of Your Storage Space

Even when simplifying, we will still have some items that will require storage. These often include seasonal items, and you will use them again when that holiday or season comes around. Try storing like items together, using as few storage containers as you possibly can. You might have to get creative with the packing, but the more you can fit in a box, the more space you will save. Also, try to make sure that all of your storage containers are the same size. This will make them easy to stack and create a cleaner and simpler appearance to your storage area.

Even though your personal areas are not seen on a regular basis, they still need to be simplified and cut back in order to make your home much more breathable. Closets and storage areas can quickly be torn into and cause the rest of the home to feel cluttered again. Don't let your personal space clutter your common space. This will only set you up for a vicious cycle that will see no end!

Chapter 4- Tips for Simplifying Your Decor

You may have a lot of personal family memories that you want to display in your home. However, there is a point where your décor can become a little too much. Clutter can happen on your walls and shelves, making it hard to see past the stuff and enjoy the simplicity of life. If you cannot see the wall behind the pictures and decorations, you probably have too much going on. Everyone walking into your home is probably on sensory overload. Would you want to walk into a place that has too much going on?

It might be time for you to put some of those memories away and simplify your décor. Think about walking into your home and what you would really like for it to look like. Do you enjoy having a simple and eye-pleasing décor? Then try to make your home reflect this idea. In this chapter, we are going to take a look at some ways that you can still hold onto some of those family memories while simplifying your home décor.

Make a Photo Collage

Many people have family photos that they wish to display on their walls. However, if you have a large family or multiple photos, this could be a quick way to clutter your walls and make for sensory overload for whoever views them. If you really want to keep these pictures on display, then try creating a photo collage of them. You can group photos by event, person, or any other them and put them in a collage frame.

This will solve the problem of wall clutter and still give you the benefit of displaying your beloved photos.

Repurpose Your Favorite Decoration Pieces

As you find yourself simplifying your living area and décor, try altering your favorite decorations so that they have a new and fresh feel to them. You might have a wreath that you can add a few baubles to and make it feel updated and different. Being creative with your décor can offer you a simpler look while cutting back on the clutter that is in your home. Reusing and refreshing what you have in creative ways can make your home feel more unique.

Change Your Theme

If you find that your current theme jumped out of the seventies, you may want to consider a change. While some people appreciate bright colors and vivid décor, the simpler you make it, the more inviting it will be. It's okay to have a few accent pieces, but make sure that your main theme is simple. Again, this is easy to accomplish by using earth tones as your color base and building around that. You don't have to add too much to your room to make it classy. In fact, a lot of people think that the less a room has, the better that it looks! Not only are you saving yourself clutter, you are also saving yourself some time when it comes to cleaning a wide array of unnecessary items. This is time that you can do what you enjoy with!

Reupholster Your Furniture

You don't have to get rid of your favorite sofa just because the coloring isn't simple and doesn't fit your décor. Try reupholstering it to make it fit into your room and making it simple. This will give you the simple and fresh feel you desire without giving up what you love. A simple pattern can help your home feel fresh and uncluttered. Try looking at this possibility before you invest in all new furniture!

Bring in Natural Elements

In a simple life, you don't want your home to feel too complex in any way. This includes your possessions and your décor. Try bringing in the feeling of nature into your home. Use natural light when possible, and get rid of anything that feels unnecessary and cluttering. By getting rid of items and cutting back on what you own, you can easily allow the simplicity of natural elements to invade your space.

Minimize Your Furniture

While furniture may be a great convenience, it can also be a great burden. It takes up space, might not even be used, and it might just cause clutter in your home. For example, my spouse loves books. We have numerous bookshelves in our living room. I know that he will never read all of those books. By getting rid of these books and bookshelves, I can really cut back the clutter in my living room and simplify my living space. Now, I just need to convince him that he doesn't need all those books…

Minimize Your Decorations

I love bric a brac and anything cute that can adorn my shelves. However, when I decided to cut back on this type of items, my home felt less cluttered. While some of these items are sentimental to me, most of them have no value whatsoever. By getting rid of most of my unnecessary and cluttering decorations, I found that I actually enjoy my home more than I did before. I can still enjoy the cute in passing, but I won't bring in home anymore to adorn my shelves.

Cutting back on your décor and simplifying what you do have are great ways to simplify your life and feel like you live for more than stuff. Keeping your possessions and your home simple will help you to focus on more important aspects of your life. Plus, the simpler your home is, the easier it is to clean! That is incentive enough for me to simplify!

Chapter 5- Tips for Organizing Your Storage Areas

Most of us don't believe that we have enough storage for the items that we wish to store. We may look at areas such as our garage, our linen closets or even our bedroom closets and think that it looks like a tornado has ripped through them. Finding places to put things will ultimately lead to clutter, and clutter is a huge eyesore. Plus, when we wish to find something, we will tear apart our storage area until we locate it.

In order to downsize, we must get rid of this clutter. This can mean giving items up to thrift stores, having a garage sale or using them as hand me downs. However you decide that you want to downsize and cut back, you will be glad you did once you see the space you have found. However, for the items that you wish to continue to store, organization can play a key factor in making sure that your home doesn't become a tornado when you want to find just one item. In this chapter, I'm going to cover some creative storage organization ideas that might help you to feel like it isn't a catch all.

Hooks and Shelves

Once you have decluttered your storage areas, it is important that you find ways to organize it so that it won't create problems for you in the future. In your storage closets, attics and garages, try using shelves and hooks on the walls to help you organize what you wish to store. By having everything in a certain place, you will take the guess work out of finding an item when you actually need it. Shelves can help accommodate your storage in multiple ways because they can be placed in such a way that you can put anything you wish upon them.

Hanging Items at Different Heights

Using your wall space can have great benefits to decluttering and organizing your storage areas. For items that can be hung on the wall, use hooks at different levels to help you to create a more organized and simple method to storing these items. When you wish to get an item that is hanging, you can find it much easier if it is at a different level than other items in your storage area.

Storage Bins and Drawers

Bins and drawers help out a lot in decluttering and storing items, especially those that will not work out well in boxes and hanging on walls. By investing in a few small storage bins and drawers, you can easily organize the small items that you have in your storage areas. Be careful that you continue to group like items together, making it easier for you to find them when you need them!

Labeling

In order to simplify your storage experience, try labeling your boxes, bins and drawers using a label machine or laminated cards. This will help guide you in organizing and finding what you wish to find in your storage areas. This will also help you to put your items back in the places where they belong without creating more clutter in your life. Why not prevent your simple and decluttered home from returning to its original state?

Categorize Your Stored Items

Once you have your items in boxes and labeled, it's important that you put like items together. For example, you will want to store seasonal decorations apart from winter clothing. This will allow you to know where to find what you want when you go looking for it. Don't make simplifying your life difficult and frustrating!

Make Use of Your Space

When you store items, it's important that you make use of the space given without cluttering it. Evaluate your storage area and determine how you can stack, build shelves, or install hooks in order to make your storage experience as pain free as possible.

Organizing and decluttering your storage space can really help you simplify your life in many ways. Not having to spend hours searching for one item or having to rip apart the closet will make it worth it for you in the long run. By cutting back and organizing, you are simplifying your life in ways that will help you for years to come.

Chapter 6- Tips for Simplifying Your Closets

As I write this book, I'm thinking about my bedroom closet. It looks like a clothing store threw up and the shoes were the unfortunate victims of an explosion. As much as I would like to say that my closet is organized by garment type and color, that would be a lie. How can I possibly make my closet look like it would be featured on television? No matter how many times I have tried to organize this area of my home, the end result remains the same. I still end up with a mess.

For this chapter, I turn to other resources for ideas on how to make my closets more organized keep them that way. Some of the ideas I will be soon trying out in my own situation. I will also provide some tips on how to organize other closets in your home. Let's try some of these tips and see if we can achieve more organized and simply closets!

Layering Hangers

I have seen this suggestion in multiple places. What you do is take soda can tabs and place them over the hook of a hanger. You can then hang another hanger from the tab, allowing you to store more than one garment and not take up closet space. This can come in handy when it comes to storing outfits, putting the top on the top hanger and the pants on the lower hanger.

Have Shelving for Your Shoes

If you have a lot of shoes, then having shoe shelves in your closet can have a huge effect on how organized your closet looks and will make it feel less cluttered. When looking for a pair of shoes, if you have shelves, you can easily view what you have instead of digging through a huge pile and creating a larger mess.

Store Only What Your Closet is Intended for

While it might feel convenient to store whatever you want to get out of sight in your bedroom closet, all you are accomplishing is creating clutter and making your closet a catch all. Make your closet for your clothing and shoes only. By limiting what you are storing in your closet to what needs to be there, you are stopping yourself from dealing with another annoying clutter situation in the future.

Get Rid of Unnecessary Items

If you haven't worn it or used it in six months, get rid of it. The number one cause of clutter is keeping something that we believe that we will use again, when in reality, we probably won't. Donate your unworn clothing, shoes, and linens to thrift shops so that they can benefit others. Not only are you solving your clutter problem, you are preventing yourself from facing future clutter problems. Plus, you are simplifying your life by being able to know what you have and where it is.

Employ Plastic Drawers

Plastic drawers in closet spaces are a nice way to do away with the dresser. You can hang most of your clothing and store what you can't in plastic drawers. These are easy to see into, and they will help you remain organized in your closet area. You can also use these to store bathroom and jewelry items to help you in finding them when needed.

Have an Organizational Method that will Allow You to Return All Items to the Same Place

While you may think that your organization will last for a while, it will quickly go back to what it was if you don't put your items back where they belong. Having a place for everything and putting everything in its place may seem cliché, but it really can help you to maintain a simple life. Once you have an organizational system that you like, find ways to put your items back and keep them where they need to be. This will not only save you time, it will save you the trouble of having to reorganize on a regular basis. While it might seem like an inconvenience to return items to their places all the time, just think of the time that it took you to organize it in the first place!

Since closets can easily become a catch all for things we wish to not see, having a way to organize them and keep them from becoming cluttered can be a huge help in making sure that your efforts are not in vain. Make sure that you use your closets for their intended purposes, whether it be for clothing or for linens. When other items make their way into these areas, it is bound to lead to clutter. Make your life simpler by changing your habits and keeping your decluttered area continuously decluttered!

Chapter 7- Downsizing for Your Sanity

When we have too much stuff, stuff can overtake our lives. It may not seem that way, but when you have to give up your enjoyment and favorite activities to organize and declutter your home, you are losing out on a life that you really deserve to be living. I don't think I have ever met a person who enjoys cleaning and organizing their home. This task is an as necessary task, and it usually gets performed about once a year. It is time consuming and frustrating.

You might want to ask yourself why you are stressing out over material possessions. After all, they mean very little to you in the grand scheme of things, so why put your time and effort into gaining and keeping them? The less you have, the happier you will be. Also, the less you have, the easier it is to keep your home clean and organized. Just thinking about these aspects of decluttering makes me want to jump up and start shoving unnecessary items into boxes for donation!

Getting rid of your unnecessary junk will help you to cut back on the stuff that causes you such a headache when it comes to cleaning and organizing. Since we have become so used to living for material possessions, we often miss out on the most important things in our lives. Don't allow stuff to take your life away. Get rid of it and simplify your life. Yes, you will still need items to live, but what you have probably is much more than what you really need.

You only have one life to live, so you need to make the most of it. If you find that your time is centered on possessions, then it's time for you to cut back and simplify. I have just started this process myself, and I have found the work that I have already done very rewarding. By cutting back on my possessions and simplifying my home, I have found that it is more aesthetically pleasing and I have less cleaning and upkeep to worry about. Having less stuff means that I don't have to clean it! I love that about living a simpler life!

Also, having a home and a life that you dream of is a goal that is well worth reaching. No one wants to look at their home and see visions of hoarders. It's just stuff, and you cannot take it with you when you die. So, what's the point in living for it? Take time to live your life and do the things that you enjoy. Allow your relationships to grow and spend time with those you care about. Don't allow your home and your possessions to stand in the way of living the life that you dream of.

If you haven't started to declutter and cut back on your possessions, I highly encourage you to. Take the time and get rid of what you don't need and limit what you do need. Get yourself organized and keep yourself that way. I assure you that once you find the simple life, you will love it and won't think about building up your stock of possessions again.

It could help your mindset to have a life that is free from clutter and free from worries about the clutter. Why not try to cut back and simplify? You might find that you enjoy your life much more once you make this change!

Conclusion

Thank you again for downloading this book!

I hope this book was able to help you to find ways to declutter and simplify your life. People live for possessions without even realizing it. Why not live for something meaningful and place the junk aside?

The next step is to find ways to cut back and simplify in your home or office. By getting rid of the extras, you will find that you will enjoy your life much more!

DOWNSIZING YOUR LIFE AND LOVING IT

50 CREATIVE WAYS TO DECLUTTER YOUR SPACE, LIVE WITH LESS AND SIMPLIFY YOUR LIFE

KATHY STANTON

Introduction

I want to thank you for downloading the book, *Downsizing Your Life and Loving It: 50 Ways to Declutter Your Space, Live with Less and Simplify Your Life.*

This book contains proven steps and strategies on how to minimalize your belongings, chore list, and thoughts in order to give you a more fulfilling and simplistic life. If you're like most people, you probably have way more than you really need. This isn't limited to possessions, but chores and thoughts. In a society where more is emphasized, living simple is difficult.

Have you found that you have way too much going on in your life? You find that your possessions outnumber your needs and you have a to do list that stretches on and on. Your life is consumed. Have you ever thought of what it would feel like to have less? If you could minimalize your stresses, would you? This book focuses on ways to simplify your life so that you can reduce stress and love life.

Thanks again for downloading this book, I hope you enjoy it!

Chapter 1- What is Too Much in Life?

Have you noticed that this society emphasizes success by how much you have rather than happiness? I have found that I hate the fact that my success is based upon how much I have. Sure, it might be nice to have the new gadgets and everything you could possibly want, but in the end, is it really worth it? No possession or amount of activity can really satisfy your need for success.

Success is defined differently for different people. Sure, some might thrive off of having more and more. However, our human nature isn't dependent upon having excess. We have simple needs that we need met, but beyond that, everything is just considered a luxury. When we make our luxuries into needs, then we tend to be unhappy.

I have evaluated my life and found that getting rid of the extras makes me feel happier. I'm not stressed out with trying to obtain more and what I have is sufficient. When I finally came to that mindset, it was a huge relief. I didn't feel like I needed to do everything in order to accomplish a goal that wasn't even necessary.

How about you? Do you find that you're stressed out by thinking about all you have to do in order to maintain what you have? Take a close look at your life. Do you have excess that you're trying to maintain? Are there things that you can do without? If your answer to any of these questions is "yes," I encourage you to read this book and reevaluate what is really a need as opposed to what is a luxury. What you might find out about yourself might surprise you.

If you're looking to simplify your life, I encourage you to continue reading. In this book, I'm going to give you some hints and tips on how to get rid of the excess so that you can enjoy what you have. You might find that the simple life is the way to go and love it as much as I do!

Chapter 2- Evaluating Need versus Want

The first step to finding a simple life is looking at what is before you. Some things you have you would consider a need, while other things are considered clutter and could easily be done away with. For some, they consider things as needs what others would easily be able to get rid of. Since every person is different, I want to look at the criteria for what a need is as opposed to a want. I'm not saying it's wrong to have items you want. However, when your life becomes dependent on keeping a certain standard of life that is unnecessary, then it becomes a stress for you and an inhibitor to the simple lifestyle.

So, I encourage you to be brutally honest with yourself when looking at the items in your life. If you find that you have more of what you want than what you actually need, you might want to reevaluate your priorities in order to simplify your life.

When Was the Last Time I Used It?

This is a big question for me. The items that I think that I need usually end up sitting in a drawer or closet. When I bought them, I thought that they would be useful, but in the end, I never even used them! Do you find things in your home that you have lightly or never used? I would consider these things a want rather than a need. These are the items that I would try to weed out of my life first.

Do I Really Want to Put the Extra Effort into Maintaining it if I Don't Need it?

Some people thrive upon having luxurious items. They are willing to work hard for them, and they will do whatever they can to keep them. However, some of these things are just not worth the effort. For example, you have a car that you really like, but it tends to break down a lot. You spend a lot of time and money trying to keep it in working order. When asked whether or not you consider this a need, you would say yes. So, you are willing to put forth the extra effort and time to maintain your luxury. If it is something that you really want and would consider a need, then by all means, keep it.

If I were to Toss it Out, Would I Miss It?

Before I decided to simplify my life and home, I would constantly come across items that I had no idea I even owned. They were probably some impulse buy that I thought that I would use later. However, they soon ended up getting stored and forgotten about. I need to ask myself when I encounter such objects one pressing question; "Will I miss it if it were not here?" For most of these things, it would be a resounding "YES!" For others, I really did need it, but ultimately forgot to use it. In a busy, cluttered life, that sometimes happens.

Does it Make Me Happy?

In the previous chapter, we talked about success and happiness and how people tend to connect the two with belongings. So, at this time, I want you to look at some of you major belongings and ask yourself whether or not they make you happy. For the most part, I bet that most of the answers will be "no." General happiness is not dependent upon what you have, but on the other factors in your life and how they all work together.

If I Were to Have Nothing, What Would I Need to Survive?

Let's do a little test. Imagine that your home was destroyed in some freak natural disaster. You literally have nothing to your name except the clothing on your back. What would you need at that point in time? Thing about the basic pyramid of needs. You probably would be thinking about food, shelter, and other practical items that would help you to survive. Odds are, you won't be thinking about replacing your laptop or the earrings that your husband gave you for your anniversary. What you have just evaluated was what is a true need as opposed to a luxury. You can live without a laptop computer and jewelry. You can't live without food or shelter.

The next time you look around your home, ask yourself some of these questions. You might be surprised at the sheer volume of goods that you own that you really could live without. Try making a change to a simple life by weeding out the luxuries and focusing on the needs. In the following chapters, I'm going to give you hints on how to simplify your life in a few different ways. Items are not the only things that keep us from enjoy simple living!

Chapter 3- How to Reduce Your Belongings

As highlighted in the previous chapter, our belongings tend to be the number one thing that keeps us from having a simple life. Even though they are just stuff, we tend to form emotional bonds with this stuff that can be difficult to break.

However, it might be necessary to break these bond if you're looking to simplify your life. This can take some time and patience on your part. No one wants to admit that something that they really like is nothing more than a thing. So, I'm going to give you some tips and hints on how to reduce your belongings in order to live a happier life.

Go Through Everything You Own

Depending upon how much you own, this can be quite the undertaking. However, it will be necessary in order to downsize your belongings to a manageable level. The first thing that I recommend is that you go through each and every item you own. Take a close look at them, and separate them into piles. Have a pile for what you will for sure keep, one for the maybes, and one to get rid of. Do this room by room so that your house won't look like a total and complete wreck. The items that you can safely say that you need to keep can be put back right away and you can evaluate the rest of it later on.

Evaluate whether what you have before you is needed

This is a test of your will. Take some time and look at your stuff. Ask yourself whether or not you really need the item and whether or not you will ever use the item on a regular basis. Imagine how your life would be without it. If you can safely say that you really don't need it, get rid of it. It's better to be honest with yourself and do it all at once than finding out later that you kept something around that resulted in clutter.

Donate or Sell Your Excess Stuff

This is another necessary part to your puzzle. Now is the time to get rid of the items that you have decided that you don't need. I prefer to donate them to a thrift store or have a garage sale. For some, donating it is the easiest option. For me, I enjoy having a yearly garage sale and getting rid of things. Not only does it make me money, but I also have the chance to invite friends or family to bring their stuff and it's like a reunion. However, arranging a garage sale can be time consuming and stressful if you don't go about it in the right way.

Have Someone Help You

Some people refuse to seek help. However, if you're living with others, they need to be on the same page as you, so enlisting their help will be necessary. Even if you live alone, having a friend come over and help you to get rid of some unnecessary stuff can both be fun and helpful. You never know, your friend might just take some of that stuff off of your hands for you and that's one less worry later on!

Asking for help is not a sign of weakness. It's simply saying that you want to make a change and that you want another person to be a part of that change. So, don't worry about someone thinking you're weak for asking for help. You're just trying to do what is best for you.

Give it to Family or Friends

Having younger (or older) siblings can be another fun way to get rid of your unwanted belongings. For me, I have a sister who loves my tastes in clothing and home décor, so when I asked if she wanted to come over and take some of the items I was getting rid of, she was excited. You might have a friend who is like that for you. Knowing someone who shares your tastes is a good way to recycle some of the old stuff you intend to get rid of. If you have some family or friends who would love to relieve you of your excess belongings, don't be afraid to ask them! It could benefit both of you.

Be Heartless

This is one tip that has helped me along the way. Since I base a lot of emotional value on some of my belongings, when I go to get rid of them, I find that I doubt my decision based upon that bond. It could be something that I got with my mother that brings back memories. However, this is something I have to look past. Look at the item for what it is. Will you need it or use it? Can you live without it? Be heartless and rip the memories that are associated with object away from it. In the end, it's just a piece of stuff that will clutter your home. Remember that!

If You Haven't used it in Six Months, Trash it

Another great method that I use to declutter my home is to look at what is before me and evaluate whether or not I have used this item in the past six months. If I haven't used or looked at it that long, I haven't missed it. I will put it into my donation pile. The biggest mistake that you can make is to look at the object and tell yourself that you will use it again. You won't, so don't keep it around. Six months is a reasonable time span to realize whether or not you will actually use it.

Downsize Your Home

For some of us, we live in a home that is much too big for our needs. If possible, downsize your living quarters to something that is more manageable to clean and furnish. I understand that moving is not feasible for all, but if you have the opportunity to downsize your home, you will also be forced to get rid of some of your belongings when you move. Think about it. This might be the way to go!

Downsizing your possessions can be a tough and time consuming process. No one likes to get rid of their things. After all, you chose them and worked hard to buy them. However, when your life becomes complicated because of your need to maintain your possessions, you're not going to be happy. Try decluttering and downsizing in the area of your possessions and see how much better you feel by making this change.

This is a process. Don't overwhelm yourself with getting rid of all the items you don't need at once. This will make the whole idea seem even more overwhelming than just keeping the stuff in your life. So, I recommend that you take this process in pieces. It could take you a few months to make it through. However long it takes, know that you're making a positive step towards simplifying your life with the shedding of your excess possessions.

Chapter 4- Cutting Back on Your Chore List

Another good way to encourage simple living is by cutting back on the list of things that you feel you have to have done. People tend to put too much on themselves, making it more difficult to have time for what really matters. Depending on your lifestyle and personality, you will value your time differently. If you feel like you're spending too much time doing mundane chores, then maybe it's time to reevaluate your priorities and make time for what really matters instead of filling your time with nonsense.

In this chapter, I am going to give you some hints as to how to cut out chores from your busy schedule in order to make more time for what really matters to you. So, if you would like to simplify your time, then let's take a look at some ways to make that happen!

Does it Really Need to be done?

Some tasks are necessary in order to run your household. Others are simply fillers. When you look at your day and the list that you have compiled that you want to get done, think about whether or not the task must get done in order to maintain your life, or if it's something that you choose to do.

By being honest with yourself and realizing that you're picking up too much on your to do list, you will be on your way to saying that some tasks are unnecessary and clutter your time.

Can You Have Someone Else do it?

When did it become a fact that you do all the chores? If you live with multiple people, this is unfair and stressful to you. Take a look at your day as opposed to the others you live with.

Can someone else do the task on the list? If you're like me and try to do it all, then there is definitely someone who will be able to help you by taking on the task and completing it. So, the next time you feel overwhelmed by the to do list, think about this factor. Have someone help you!

What Would you do with Some Free Time?

Feel free to daydream a little bit. What would you do if you found some extra free time within your day? Well, by simplifying your chore list, you might be able to make this daydream a possibility. Don't be afraid to think about how you would spend your time if you didn't have a million things to do. It can really work out that you can have that time if you learn to manage your time properly and leave out unnecessary tasks.

What Activities Would You Like to Spend Your Time Doing?

Going along with the question above, think about ways you would like to spend your time. You probably don't want to be spending great amounts of time working in order to maintain a luxurious lifestyle that you could easily do without. Surprisingly enough, people do this every day. They work hard in order to buy things and do things that they cannot afford. It's okay to do some things you want to do, but don't make it so extreme that you end up working more than you need to in order to get there!

Respect Your Time and That of Others

In today's world, we look out for number one and try to focus on helping everyone else at the same time. If you're one of these people, you will give your time to help anyone in need. This can be a positive thing, but it can easily turn into something negative. People who realize that you will do whatever you want them to do will use you for that reason. They will have little regard for your time, but focus on what you can do for them. On the flip side, you might be that person who expects that from others. The biggest tip I can give here is respect your own time and that of others. Once you learn that your time is valuable and their time is too, you will be finding that you can maintain a healthier balance in your schedule.

Plan What is Necessary and Leave Out the Unnecessary

Life is unpredictable. I get that. However, having a plan to your day can be very helpful in making sure that you accomplish the necessary tasks. Other stuff will come up throughout the day. Take it as it comes. However, if you're planning on doing things that are not necessary for you, then you are filling your day with clutter. The point it to get away from this clutter so that you can have a healthy and happy life.

Don't Allow Others' Opinions of You to Dominate Your Time and Your Lifestyle

People are opinionated beings. If you ask every person in your life for suggestions on how to live yours, you will get as many answers as people. They aren't living your life though. You are. So, when you begin to think about what someone else is going to think about what you're doing, let those thoughts slip away. If you live your life based upon someone else's opinions, you're not living your own life, but theirs. Let them live the way they want and you live the way you want. Don't allow other people's opinions to dictate how you live your life.

By making some changes to your schedule and what you choose to do on a daily basis, you can simplify your life and make yourself happier because you will have more time to do what you want to do. Your schedule is a huge part of your day, so being able to cut out the unnecessary factors will make it easier for you to have time for what you would like to do and spend time with those who you value.

Time is a tricky thing. We find ourselves wasting it frequently and then wishing we could have it back. If you find that you tend to waste more time than using it productively, try to make some changes to your schedule that will open up time for what is necessary and what you would enjoy doing.

Chapter 5- Simplifying Your Thought Life

If you're anything like me, then your mind is always running on overdrive. When I'm not thinking about one thing, another thought consumes my mind. There is no peace when you are constantly thinking. Have you ever tried to simplify your thoughts so that you can have a peaceful existence? It is impossible, but you will need to learn to train your brain to make it happen. This can be done in a number of ways, but depending on how you operate, you might find one way works much better than another.

In this chapter, I'm going to give you some advice on how to simplify your thoughts in order to downsize the amount of stress in your life. When you have tranquil thoughts, then you will be able to have a less stressful and turbulent existence.

Meditate

When you find that you cannot concentrate on anything because your mind is so consumed with other thoughts, take a moment out of your time and meditate. There are a number of things that you can meditate on. Think about your religion, your friends, your family, or even your pets. Find something that will center you when you begin to feel your mind go out of control. By focusing on this, the random and irritating thoughts will ease themselves out of your mind and you can focus on the tasks at hand.

Prayer

If you follow a religion, praying is a great way to focus your energy and thought process. By taking a few moments and talking to God, you will find that you will feel yourself calm down and that the thoughts will go away. When you have too much going on in your head, taking time to let some of that stress out is helpful to your happiness and to your thoughts.

Push the Negative Thoughts Away

Some people find that the thoughts that flood their minds are negative and self-defeating. If you're the type of person who tends to have a negative thought life, then it's time to put those thoughts aside and let positive ones in. It's difficult to break a bad habit of negative thinking once it begins. However, try to break the pattern by pushing those negative thoughts out of your head and trying to replace them with happier thoughts. You will never have a happy life if your mind is cluttered by negative thoughts!

Focus on the Moment

Focus is one of the ways that you can make your thought processes simpler and more fulfilling. I find that I tend to let my mind wander when the topic of my focus isn't exciting or thought-provoking. However, if I were to focus on the moment, I would get that task done quicker and then I would have time to think about other things. If you lack focus on what you need to do, then you will only draw out the process and make it longer than it really needs to be.

Push Away the "What if" Mentality

I'm a daydreamer and I will admit that. However, I will keep myself awake at night thinking about what would happen if I would have done something differently. Don't beat yourself up about what has already happened. If your thoughts are consumed by this type of thinking, it's time for you to break that habit. The what ifs will only make you miserable and rob you of time that you could be spending doing other tasks.

Stop Random Thinking When it Begins

If your mind tends to wander, then try to stop it from going to places it doesn't need to be before it has a chance to go there. There are certain triggers that will get me to start thinking about random circumstances. Once I identified these triggers,

I was able to stop the random thoughts before they even had a chance to begin. Think about things that will divert your attention and recognize them if you have trouble focusing on what needs to be done. Knowing these diversions will make it easier for you to push them away when necessary.

Learn to Say No to Your Thoughts

Sometimes, random thoughts do creep in. You start by asking yourself whether or not you should go and do an activity later on. Before you know it, you will be thinking about doing this activity, the ramifications of the activity, what it will entail, and any number of thoughts that surround it. However, you're supposed to be focused on another task. That task is being pushed aside for your random thoughts. So, learn how to say no to your thoughts when you notice that they can lead you down a path that will lead to distraction. If the thought is important, jot it down and come back to it when you have time to think about it.

Life tends to be more complicated when we think more than we should about things we shouldn't be thinking about. We all do it. Depending on how you handle the thoughts and choose to get rid of them will determine your mind's declutter process. Yes, your mind can be just as cluttered as your schedule or your home. By learning to simplify your thought process, you will discover that you will have more freedom to get what needs to be done accomplished and have time to do what you would like to do afterwards.

Thoughts are a difficult territory to control. We are used to our thoughts taking us wherever they want to, and trying to tell them they can't do that can be a long and frustrating process. However, you will find that simplifying your thoughts will increase your ability to lead a simple and happier lifestyle.

Chapter 6- Enjoying what Matters

If you have found that you don't have much time to enjoy your life, then it's quite possible that you have too much stuff going on. Whether it be too much stuff or too many thoughts, something is making it so that you cannot enjoy what really matters to you. It might take some time to figure out what is making your life so complicated and stressful, but once you do, you will be able to make the necessary changes in order to live a simpler, more fulfilling life.

After discussing how to rid yourself of all the extra stuff in your life, I'd like to take this chapter to focus on how to enjoy what matters to you once you have cleared out the clutter of life. Again, this might be a stage that will take some time to reach, but once you're there, you will be happier and more fulfilled with your life.

Plan Fun Activities with Those You Care About

Instead of cluttering your day with things that really don't matter, plan activities with friends and family that you will enjoy. Simply getting together with a friend for a cup of coffee can make your day much more enjoyable and take some of the hustle and bustle from your life. Before our society got so busy and complicated, people spent more time together. Try this and see if it will make you feel happier and more content.

Take Time to Enjoy the Moment

When our lives are busy and hectic, we don't have the opportunity to enjoy the moment for what it really is. Take that time to enjoy the beauty of a summer day while walking to work. Find things to appreciate in the small areas of life. If you can find positive things to enjoy about whatever you're doing, you will find that your life will feel more complete and more fulfilling. Like the old saying goes, "Take time to smell the roses." Take some time to enjoy the small and simple things in life.

Take Time for What You Want to Do

You might feel that you're being selfish by doing this, but by taking time to do what you enjoy can have a huge impact on your life. This can be a simple thing that you enjoy doing on a daily basis that will help you to enjoy your day. Maybe you like the extra flavored creamer in your coffee, so you use it when you feel like you might have a rough day. Whatever you want to do, give yourself the satisfaction of doing it. It will help you to enjoy your life more.

Don't Allow Others to Dominate Your Time

We talked a little about this in a previous chapter. If you're the type of person who will bend over backwards to help someone, you will get taken advantage of by the wrong people. When that happens, they will dominate your time with their needs and you won't have time to take care of your own needs. This is not only robbing you of your time, but it also enables them to use others instead of being self-sufficient. Don't be afraid to say no to someone who obviously can fend for himself. You aren't being cruel, you're just making it so that you can have your time and the other person will learn to do for himself.

Allow Yourself the Freedom to Enjoy Your Time

I know that I find myself feeling guilty when I get time to myself. I always feel like I could be doing something else to help someone else. However, if I don't look out for myself, then I am ultimately running myself toward a condition of being burnt out. Take some time to do what you enjoy and give yourself the freedom to enjoy that time without feeling guilty. Sadly enough, most of us don't get that freedom in our lives, and it is necessary to keep ourselves happy and centered.

Learning to enjoy the changes that you make in your life is crucial to making your simple life work for you. If you make changes to your life and they go without notice, then you have wasted your time. So, when you pursue that simple life, learn to find ways to enjoy your life. Like I stated above, you can simply enjoy a walk from your car to your place of employment. It's the simple things in life that really make it more enjoyable.

One of the biggest obstacles that you will endure when trying to enjoy your time is the feeling of guilt that you're not helping someone else. The sooner you realize that you need to take care of yourself before you can help others, the sooner you will be free to enjoy a simple life and love it.

Chapter 7- Loving Your Simple Life

Life isn't meant to be complicated and stressful. We make it that way with what we choose to do with our lives. So, by realizing that your life doesn't have to be complicated, you're ready to pursue a simple and enjoyable life!

Now that you're on your way to finding out how a simple life can benefit your way of thinking and how you live your life, you can begin to enjoying your simple life. Since you're so used to making decisions based upon a busy and full life, having time to enjoy the simple things in life might be new concept to you. What would you do if you could take a breath and enjoy life for what it is?

Let me tell you a little bit about my own experience. Now that I don't have the stress of providing a lifestyle beyond my means, I am much happier. I love the fact that I don't have to worry about how I'm going to pay my bills, what I need to buy, and who will judge me for my simple life. Since I have found that we tend to put on a show for the rest of the world, not doing so has made a huge impact on how I enjoy my life. It's my life and no one else's opinions matter.

Once you take the next step and realize that you don't need the world to be happy, you will be on your way to finding your happiness. By getting rid of all the excess, you are actually gaining more. You will have more time, more quality to your relationships, and less stress. Those all sound great, right?

If you haven't thought about pursuing a simpler lifestyle, then I encourage you to give it a try. There are many people I know of who are taking the next steps to getting rid of the excess in their lives and I can already see a difference in their lives. They just seem happier and more fulfilled.

Take the chance at being happy. Downsize and see how it can benefit you. I'm living a simple lifestyle and loving it, and I'm sure you will too if you will give it a chance. Good luck!

Conclusion

Thank you again for downloading this book!

I hope this book was able to help you to find ways to simplify your life through getting rid of unnecessary thoughts, possessions, and chores. We tend to make our lives much more complicated without meaning to. By having a simple life, we can learn to enjoy our lives much more.

The next step is to figure out areas in your life that are complicated. By knowing what you would like to change about your life, you will be prepared to take steps to simplify your day and love it!

Finally, if you enjoyed this book, then I'd like to ask you for a favor, would you be kind enough to leave a review for this book on Amazon? It'd be greatly appreciated!

CHEAPSKATE LIVING AND LOVING IT

50 CREATIVE WAYS TO SAVE MONEY, LIVE A FRUGAL LIFESTYLE AND ENJOY LIFE DEBT FREE

KATHY STANTON

Introduction

I want to thank you and congratulate you for downloading the book, *"Cheapskate Living And Loving It"*.

This book contains proven steps and strategies on how to Save Money, Live a Frugal Lifestyle and Enjoy Life Debt Free.

Today many people are struggling just to make ends meet but you do not have to be one of those people! With the tips you will learn in this book, you will be living the life you always dreamed of and doing it debt free! You are going to learn not only how to save money every single day, but you are going to learn my proven strategy on how to pay off all of your bills and get out of debt.

There are tips in this book for every single person and along with the tips you will find explanations on how to follow through, as well as how much money you will be able to save each year by following these tips. If you choose to implement just a few of the tips in this book, you will find yourself saving hundreds of dollars each year that you can put toward getting out of debt and staying debt free!

The frugal lifestyle is a great one, so don't feel like you are going to have to do without the things you love just to save money. I am going to show you how to enjoy all of the things you do right now but save as much money as you can in the process!

Thanks again for downloading this book, I hope you enjoy it!

Chapter 1

Saving Money on Your Grocery Bill

Groceries are one of the largest bills that many of us have to budget for each month. It is not a luxury item that we can choose to live without, but there are tons of ways for you to save on your grocery bill each week!

1. Start clipping coupons. Every year companies send out millions of dollars worth of coupons, but only a fraction of them are used. If you take just one hour each week and start clipping coupons, you will find that you will be able to buy name brand foods for much cheaper than you would pay for even the store brands. At first, this is going to cost you a few dollars per week but in the long run it is going to pay off substantially.

   Now, I want to explain that along with our food we usually buy our household supplies as well as our toiletries, so that is going to be part of what you will save money on with coupons.

   The first thing you are going to do is to collect your coupons. You can print these offline or clip them out of your Sunday paper. There are even sites online where you can purchase inserts for as low as 25 cents each plus shipping. This makes it a lot cheaper than buying a Sunday paper, which usually runs about $2.50 on average.

If you have a large family to feed, you will be able to purchase multiple inserts to save you a ton of money. Now, many people will clip a few coupons and go out to the local store and use them right away. You are not going to do this. You are going to save your coupons for when there is a sale and stock up on that item for free or almost free.

You need to stock up enough of that item to get you through about 6 weeks, which is when the item will go on sale again. Here is an example that is using hygiene products, there was a specific brand name shampoo and conditioner that was on sale at my local store. The normal price was $3.50 per bottle but it was on sale for $2.50 a bottle.

I knew I had ten $5 off two bottle coupons, so I ended up getting 10 shampoos and 10 conditioners absolutely free. Another one that I just took advantage of was a very expensive lotion that was on sale at my store for $3.00 per bottle. I had ten $5 off two coupons which made them 50 cents a piece, but to top that off I had a coupon that gave me $5 off a purchase of $25 or more making 20 lotions absolutely free!

You can do this on food just like you can on body products, cleaning products, and laundry supplies. Wait for a sale, top it with a coupon and get the lowest price possible!

2. Grocery shop at your local dollar store. I am talking about your dollar store that sells everything for a dollar! They sell groceries there too. They also take coupons, which makes everything very cheap. For example, they sell cereal at my local dollar store. Cereal for a dollar is great, but throw a coupon on top of that and get it for 66 cents a box, now that is amazing!

3. Plan your meals each week and use your grocery store flyer to do so! Every week you should get your grocery store flyer in the mail, use this along with your coupons to decide what you are going to eat for the week. Write down all the ingredients you will need for you meals planning them around what is on sale.

4. Shop in your own pantry. This is a big one! So many times people do not realize what they actually have in their cabinets. Have you ever went to the store, saw something you thought you needed, bought it only to come home and find 3 of the exact same untouched product in your cabinet? Once you have created your list of all the ingredients you will need for the week, check your pantry to see if you have any of them already in there.

5. Cook once, eat three times. This is one of my favorites. Did you know that you could actually get three meals for a family of four out of just one chicken? This is how I do it; first, I boil the cut up chicken to make chicken and dumplings with. I remove all the meat from the bones after the chicken has boiled; use the stock to make my dumplings adding about 1/3 of the meat. Then, I put the bones and skin in the crock-pot to make chicken noodle soup stock. Finally, I am able to throw some barbeque sauce on the 2/3 chicken meat I have left and serve barbequed chicken sandwiches.

You can do this with tons of different foods and cut back on what you are paying for meat each week!

6. Find a local discount grocery store. Many people like to say that the food you are buying at a discount grocery store is no good and you will get sick if you eat it. That in fact is not true. Each week I load up my children and drive 50 miles to the closest discount grocery store. The reason is that I am able to literally triple my money I have budgeted for groceries. For example, I am able to buy whole frozen organic chickens for no more than $3. Now I have told you how we can make one chicken last three days, so it is costing me $1 a day for our chicken!

You can purchase everything you need at a discount grocery store! They sell milk way cheaper than you will ever find at the grocery store and it is not out of date. They sell a 24 case of yogurt for 2 bucks! Check around and see if you have a discount grocery store near you, even if you have to drive a little ways, it is worth it because you will be saving more than you can imagine on your grocery bill.

7. So many times, we have leftovers after dinner and think nothing about throwing them in the trash. If you really want to save money, you need to rethink leftovers. Make them into something different, take them for

lunch the next day look at those leftovers as your money, don't throw your money away. There are even times I purposely make leftovers because I know we can eat it on another night or I plan to make it into something else. Another great thing my kids love to do is leftover day. We save what is leftover throughout the week, throw it in the freezer, then on Sunday have a buffet type meal with all types of choices. This ensures nothing goes to waste.

8. Stop snacking or allowing children to graze while they are at home. So much food can disappear if you allow your children to get in the pantry and eat whenever they feel like it. You need to set up a schedule because the fact is that children as well as many adults will eat simply because the food is there and they can.

9. Set a budget and stick to it. If you set a budget and stick to it you will learn very quickly how to stretch you money. I am not joking when I say stick to it. If you go shopping on Saturdays and run out of food on Thursday, you will learn how to stretch whatever is left in your cabinets and you will be much more cautious the next week.

10. Only go to the store once a week and go with a list. Never go in the store without a list of the items you intend to buy. If you do, you will find that you are over spending and not getting the food that you really need to prepare meals with. Take your list and don't allow temptation to overtake you. Never go to the store just to pick up one or two things once you have already done your weekly shopping. So many times, we go in looking for one or two items and come out with a cartload. If you forget something, make due or figure something else out, but do not go back into that store. If you absolutely have to go in, only take the amount of money needed to purchase the item you need. Leave the debit card in the car and grab a little cash.

Chapter 2

Saving Money on Your Electric Bill

Oh how we dread seeing that electric bill each and every month. There used to be times that I had no idea how much electricity I had used and felt completely helpless. That was until I received an electric bill that was more than my house payment last winter. I decided things had to change. Here are some changes you can make.

1. No more dryer! Did you know that you could lower your electric bill tremendously if you just stop using your dryer? In the spring, summer and most of the fall you can line dry your clothes outside. In the winter, you can purchase a cheap (usually around $5) drying rack for your house. These racks usually hold about one load of laundry each.

2. How many times have we been told that we should turn the heat down in our homes if we want to lower our electric bill? I was taught that you should turn it down, then if you get really cold, warm up the house and turn it back down again. Then a study came out by my local electric company that said do not set your thermostat at one temperature and leave it there unless you are going to be out of the house for several hours or are going to bed. What you can do is in the winter start with your thermostat at 68 degrees, if you are comfortable at that temperature drop it to 67. Continue to do this until you find the temperature that you just cannot stand. In my

house, we often have jackets, multiple layers or blankets on us in the wintertime.

In the summer, you want to do the opposite. Set your thermostat at 74 degrees and see how warm you can stand it. On the days that it is not extremely hot, open your windows, turn on the fans and let the summer air in your home. Most of the time during the spring and fall you should allow your windows to be open since the temperature outside is not too hot or too cold.

3. Check all of your windows and doors for gaps as well as around your baseboards if you have a basement. In older homes, this is where a lot of heat is lost and cold air comes in at. If you find gaps, fix them.

4. Close off the rooms that are not in use. Shut the doors to the rooms that no one is in. If the kids are in the living room, there is no reason to heat the bedrooms. If no one is in the bathroom, shut that door. This will keep the majority of the heat in the main part of the house near the thermostat, which will ensure your furnace is not over working and you are not wasting any heat. You can do the same thing in the summer!

5. Open your curtains in the winter and close them in the summer! Find the windows in your home that face the sun, when the sun is high in the sky, open those curtains in the winter, this will help heat your house. In the summer, it will heat your house as well so make sure you close the curtains.

6. Unplug everything! Did you know that while you sleep at night and all of your electronics are shut off, they are

still using electricity? Even that cell phone charger you leave plugged into the wall when your phone is not charging is constantly using electricity. When you finish using something, unplug it.

7. Wash your clothes in cold water. This will work for the majority of people, unless you have an extremely dirty job you should wash all of your clothes in cold water. If you have clothes that are very soiled, you should keep them separate from the rest of your clothing and wash them in hot water by themselves. You should also make sure to wash your whites in hot water at least once per month to ensure they stay bright white.

8. Remove some of the light bulbs! In my house, I have two chandeliers that hang from the ceiling, each of these takes eight light bulbs. In no way do we need eight light bulbs to light our rooms, so I only put two light bulbs in each one. True it does not have the same effect as all eight, but you will save money if you don't fill up your light fixtures.

9. Change your filters in your furnace/air conditioner every month to keep it from over working and to keep the air flowing.

10. If you have the choice between the microwave oven and your conventional oven, use the microwave, it uses 90 percent less electricity than the conventional oven. If you have to use the conventional oven open it up after you shut if off in the winter, you can use that heat that is trapped in there to warm your house.

Chapter 3

Television, Phone, Internet, Cells and More

I once found myself paying over $100 for my satellite bill, $70 for my internet, $60 for a home phone and over $100 a month for my cell phone. I was tired of wasting money on these things, so I made a few changes. Here are a few tips for you for saving money on these bills and more!

1. Cut out the satellite. There is no reason for you to pay that huge satellite bill each month, instead opt for Netflix or something like Netflix. Today there are tons of different programs you can choose from and they start at about $7 a month. Sure, you will be one season behind on the shows you watch, but really what does that matter when you are saving over $1,000 a year!

    Instead of using the video on demand service, wait and watch the movie later. There is no point in paying $5 to watch a movie once, when you can purchase it at a resale shop for $1 in just a few months and watch it whenever you want. Or just order it from Netflix. You can have your movie in the mail in just a few days!

2. The phone bill was also another huge issue for me as well as my internet bill. Now, of course you can cut these bills completely if you really do not need them, but I have to have them for my work. I went to my local phone company and talked to them about the price. I ended up being able to pay just $69 each month for both services instead of the $130 I was paying. If you don't need the internet for work or school, it is best to go ahead and have it and your home phone shut off and use only your cell phone for these services.

3. Speaking of cell phones, we can really run up a huge bill each month. The way I got rid of this bill was at my local Wal-Mart. Yes you heard me right. I went to Wal-Mart, picked up a $10 prepaid phone and started looking at plans. I do not need the internet on my phone since I have it at home, so I am able to pay $35 per month for unlimited talk and text. Now, if I needed the internet on my phone and did not have it at home, I could pay $50 per month for unlimited talk text and web. This is a huge savings over any contract you will get with a cell phone. The phones are just as good as the ones you get with a contract and you don't have to be stuck with some out of date flip phone. If you are looking to save money on your cell phone bill, check out the prepaid cell phones available in your area.

4. Consider working from home. This is a huge money saver. Before I worked from home, I had to pay a babysitter to watch my three children, I had to pay for gas to get back and forth to work and the list went on and on. Now my children stay at home with me while I work in my office, saving me over $1,200 a month plus gas and so on. Figure out if it is feasible for you to work at home and determine how much money you will save if you do.

5. Stop purchasing items you have to make payments on. If you are going to purchase a car, make sure you have

the cash to do so. The last car I purchased after searching for several hours online cost me $500. I sold my other car for $500 and paid cash for the one I own now. The car is not beat up or a rust bucket, it is a 94 Lincoln that runs like a charm. If you take the time to search for these deals, you are going to save a ton in interest in the long run.

6. Buy used and save the difference. Going along with not making payments on anything, stop buying everything brand new. Find used items and save your money. Six years ago I purchased a used washer and dryer. I am very picky about my clothes, so after 2 hours of scrubbing them out, I was ready to use them. I paid $50 total for both and they are currently in my laundry room doing a perfect job. Granted, I do not use the dryer often, but it is there when I need it. You can do this with all of your appliances, but you need to make sure you are getting a good deal. For example, I went to buy a used deep freeze. It cost $100, so I decided I wanted to compare prices with a new one and found I could get a larger one that was on sale at a local store new for $60. Don't assume just because it is being sold as used that you are getting the lowest price you can.

7. Cut up the credit cards and pay them off. I personally have never owned a credit card and I never want to. I watched my parents have to file bankruptcy due to overspending on credit cards. If you currently own a credit card, cut it up, call the company and see if they will lower your interest rate then start paying them off. Once they are paid off, do not apply for new ones. Live on what cash you have in your pocket and do not accumulate debt.

8. Consider quitting smoking and drinking. The average smoker spends over $150 each month on cigarettes and depending on how much you are drinking you could be spending upwards of $100 on that as well. That is

$3,000 a year that you can put toward something more important. Saving money and being frugal has a lot to do with being healthy as well and just imagine the amount of money you will end up saving on future doctor bills if you quit now.

9. Shop at thrift shops and yard sales. You may think that you will not find anything that you like if you purchase from thrift shops or yard sales, but the truth is you can find amazing treasures. For example, my entire living room is furnished with Ashley furniture. I bought it at a yard sale from an elderly couple. It was very well cared for and I spent a total of $200 for a couch, loveseat, and two chairs. All of the pictures in my home have come from thrift shops, as well as all of the televisions I own. You can purchase a 40-inch television from a thrift shop for about $40. This is because they usually do not have the remote with them, but guess what; you can order a universal remote from Amazon for about $10. So you end up spending around $50 for the entire thing!

10. Find things to do that do not cost any money. Often times people get bored and they decide that they want to go spend some money to entertain themselves, instead find things to do that are free. Such as a hike in the woods, visiting your local park, taking your kids swimming in the river or teaching them about volunteering at the local animal shelter. You can also watch your local paper for free events that are being held in your town such as parades, car shows or cook offs.

Chapter 4

And There is More!

There are even more ways for you to save money each and every day! I know at this point you may be getting a little overwhelmed, but choose a few money saving ideas from this book and implement them. Once you are able to do them with consistency add a few more. This is not all or nothing here. Remember, saving just a little will help you become encouraged to save even more!

1. Take advantage of end of season sales. Did you know that you can get brand name clothes brand new for literally pennies on the dollar? At the end of each season clothing goes on sale, if you watch the prices you will be able to get $100 shirts for a couple bucks! When you have growing kids this is a great way to keep them in stylish clothing without breaking the bank. What I do is purchase one or two sizes bigger than what my child is currently wearing so that the new clothes will fit when that season comes around again. You can also do this for holiday decorations, costumes, and even purchase your Christmas presents for the next year right after this years Christmas! You will end up saving about 90% on Christmas and you will be prepared for the following year!

2. Cook all of your meals at home. If you find that you are going out to eat more than once a month, you really need to think about cooking more meals at home. You see, for what you spend on one meal at a fast food place,

you could make dinner for four at home and it's going to be much more healthy.

3. If something is broken, do not throw it away, fix it! We live in a society where everything is disposable, but if you really want to save money, learn how to fix the things that are broken.

4. Rent instead of own. There are those who will disagree with this, but if you rent a house instead of purchase it, you don't have to pay home owners insurance, you don't have to worry about how you will pay for a new water heater, just call the landlord and let them deal with it.

5. Move to a smaller cheaper house. This is one that gets a lot of people. We want our children to have their own bedrooms, to have a huge house to live in and we want others to think we are well off. If you are paying for more house than you really need, you are wasting your money. I had to consider this when I was living in a five bedroom house realizing we actually only used a few of the rooms. So much space was not being used, therefore so much of my money was being wasted. Look into a smaller cheaper house if you find that all of your house is not being used.

6. Plant a garden. Gardening is very inexpensive and it can produce lots of great food for you to eat. You can also sell the excess at your local farmers market in order to make some extra cash on the side!

7. Raise your own chickens. Many people have trouble eating the chickens that they raise, so for those people, just get enough chickens to produce the number of eggs you need each day! If you have extra sell them. In the summer, you can allow your chickens to roam your yard and eat up all the bugs along with some grass to cut back on chicken feed.

8. Learn how to cut your own hair or at least your children's hair. In our house, I cut everyone's hair except my own. I have very long hair and when I want it trimmed I am willing to pay the $8 to have it done, but only once or twice a year. If you can cut your own hair that is great, if not find a low priced salon and have them do it on the cheap.

9. Dying your own hair can also save you a ton of money. With salon prices sky rocketing, you can save about $100 each time you dye your hair at home depending on how long it is.

10. Take snacks with you wherever you go. How often do you jump in the car to go somewhere and the kids start complaining that they are hungry? You end up stopping by a fast food joint and spending $40 on junk food. Instead, grab some Ziploc bags and stuff them full of healthy snacks. The next time the kids say they are, hungry hand them a bag and be on your way.

Chapter 5

Final Tips for You to Save Money!

In this next chapter, I am going to give you ten more tips to help you save money. Here are ten more tips to help save you money every day!

1. Find out if your bank is charging you fees. What happens if your bank account gets overdrawn by accident? How much do you end up paying? If you find that you are paying fees at your bank, find a bank that works for you. For example, my bank offers a plan for free that allows you to overdraw by $600 as long as you pay off the balance within a month. This is great in case there is some type of emergency and you don't have to worry about paying $30 a day in overdraft fees!

2. Have your bills automatically taken out of your bank account each month. Life is fast and sometimes we forget to send that bill or jump online to pay it, so instead of getting charged late fees each month, just sign up to auto pay your bills each month. This can save a few hundred dollars in late fees each year.

3. Sell the things you don't need! Don't give away the clothes that your children have out grown, take them to a thrift shop and sell them on consignment or better yet have a yard sale and make some extra cash. I always

send everything to the thrift shop because I don't have much time to plan a yard sale and they do all the work for me. You do need to understand they will take a percentage of what your stuff sells for though.

4. Stop buying paper towels (unless of course you have a coupon that makes them free). Instead of buying paper towels, go buy a pack of white wash cloths for $3 that you will use specifically for cleaning.

5. Freeze the items you buy in bulk. A few weeks ago I went to the local discount grocery store and they had Coffee Mate creamer on sale for 2 for a dollar. This stuff is very expensive, so I purchased several. I knew that if I did not use them quickly they would go bad, so instead, I put them in the freezer and each week I can grab one out to use. I now have enough creamer for several months and saved around $80! You can freeze tons of items you find on sale like this, and if you don't know ask someone who works at the store, they can usually tell you.

6. If you are going to run your appliances (dishwasher, washing machine, dryer) run them at night. The off peak hour prices for electricity are cheaper than during the day!

7. Save all of your change for a year. Each time you empty your pockets or your purse, put your loose change in a jar, at the end of the year deposit this change into a savings account.

8. Do you get a tax return? Many people with children get a tax return each year, many of these people also end up wasting this money on items they do not really need. Instead of wasting your tax return, create a plan to use it to pay up your bills for several months in advance, or use it to pay down some of that debt. This is a great chance for you to benefit yourself in the days to come.

9. Use a thirty-day plan. If you are in the store and you see something that you want, put it back on the shelf and wait for thirty days. If in thirty days you still want the item, see if you can fit it into your budget, but chances are you are going to forget about the item because you only wanted it on impulse.

10. Need it or want it. Many people have to realize there is a difference between need and want. They go into the store see an item they want and tell themselves they need it for this specific reason. A need is something that you will not be able to live without. A want is obviously something you can live without but would really like. Ask yourself if you really need the item before buying it.

Chapter 6

How to Get Out of Debt for Good

Throughout this book, I have given you tips on how to save money, but what are you supposed to do with the money you are saving? Of course you can put it in the bank in a savings account, but before you do that you want to get yourself out of debt.

It does not matter what kind of debt you have, the technique I am going to teach you will get you completely out of debt in the shortest amount of time possible.

First, I want you to get a pen and paper and start writing down all of the debt you own and how much you currently own on that debt. Like this:

Medical $6,543

MasterCard $4,154

Visa $2,894

Car $7,325

And so on. Now once you have your list, you are going to find the debt that you owe the least amount on. Using the above example, you would want to begin with the Visa card. If your minimum monthly payment is $200, I want you to budget that $200 into your monthly bills. I also want you to add an extra $50 to $100 onto the payment depending on how much you can afford.

Keep making your minimum payments on the rest of your bills until the Visa is paid in full. Next, you would move on to the MasterCard. Let's say you have been paying $300 a month toward that debt, I want you to take that $300 plus the $200 you were paying for your Visa as well as the $50 to $100 dollars you added on to the minimum payment and pay that all towards your MasterCard. This would make your payment $550 to $600 dollars a month.

After you have paid off your MasterCard, you are going to move on to the next bill. In this example you would begin paying off your medical bills. So, if you are paying a minimum of $100 dollars per month toward your medical bills, you are going to take the $200 you were paying toward your Visa before it was paid off, plus the $50 to $100 extra you were sending in, add to that the $300 you were paying toward your MasterCard before it was paid off, and you will be sending $650-$700 dollars per month toward your medical bills.

You will continue this process until all of your debt is paid off. Then, you will keep following the tips I have given you in this book to ensure you do not accrue more debt. It is important that you take the money you were paying toward previous bills and budget it for the next bill, because otherwise you are going to find yourself spending and wasting all of that money that should be going to bills. Once your debt is paid off, you need to set it up with your bank so the money is deposited directly into a savings account each and every month.

Doing this will ensure that you are not wasting your money, but setting up a nice nest egg for yourself and your family.

This process is simple, but depending on the amount of debt, you have it can take some time. Remember the tip I gave you about your tax return, if you do get one, you can also use this to pay down these debts making the process go much, much faster.

Chapter 7

Frugal Lifestyle

Living frugally and without debt is a lifestyle and it may take some time for you to get used to it, but it is so freeing that it is worth all of the work that goes into it. When you decide that you want to live frugally and without debt, sit down and make a list of reasons why you want to do so.

Keep this list of reasons close by so that if you start to feel like you are missing out on certain things in life you will be reminded of what your goals are. One of the rules in our house is that if we don't have a coupon for it, we do not purchase it. So, if you really are wanting something search the internet for a coupon for it or just wait until it goes on sale.

Another part of living the frugal lifestyle is taking care of the things you have and respecting what you have spent your money on. So what if you own a $50 couch, that is $50 out of your pocket, take care of it and respect it.

Finally, I want to talk to you about passing on the frugal lifestyle. How great would it feel if you could say your children would never be in debt? What about if you knew that they would never go without or want because you taught them how to save and spend money wisely. If for no other reason than this, I hope that you take the tips in this book and implement them into your life.

You must understand before you decide to make these changes, that living frugally and saving money does take some extra work in life! It does take giving up some conveniences, but trust me if you follow through with this in a few months you won't even miss them.

Now, how are you going to implement these changes? As I mentioned before, I want you to pick a few of the tips I have given you and start making those changes in your life. Once you have applied these changes, after a few weeks add a few more changes.

You don't want to make too many changes at once because if you do you will find that they are harder to stick to. Most people want to make huge changes in their lives and they fail because they really are asking too much of themselves. But if you add in small changes, you will barely notice them and you will raise your chances of being successful.

One thing that you are going to do while you are making these changes is fail. You are going to see something in the store that you really like and buy it on impulse or order something off of the internet, but when this happens don't give up, keep your head up and start again.

We as humans only learn through failure and if you fail along the way, take note of it then move on. This only gets easier as time goes on.

Conclusion

Thank you again for downloading this book!

I hope this book was able to help you to save money, get out of debt and live a more frugal life!

The next step is to get started using these tips and paying off that debt!

Finally, if you enjoyed this book, then I'd like to ask you for a favor, would you be kind enough to leave a review for this book on Amazon? It'd be greatly appreciated!

HABIT STACKING

FOR FRUGAL LIVING

50 Simple Life Changing Tips To Save Money, Get Out Of Debt And Live A Happy Life

KATHY STANTON

Introduction

I want to thank you and congratulate you for downloading the book, *Habit Stacking for Frugal Living: 50 Simple Life Changing Tips to Save Money, Get out Of Debt and Live a Happy Life*

This book contains proven steps and strategies on how to create positive habits that will help you to change your saving and spending habits. Everyone has something they would like to change about their financial situation. Some have excess credit cards while others have trouble saving their money. Whatever your struggle is, I will try to give you ideas for changing that habit.

Do you find that you're living paycheck to paycheck? When you need to get gas in your car, you discover that you don't have enough to do so? If you struggle financially, then take some time to create some new and positive habits to pull yourself out of your financial slump. This book is designed to give you ideas of habits you can implement into your daily life in order to free yourself of financial stress.

Thanks again for downloading this book, I hope you enjoy it!

Chapter 1- What Financial Habits Would You Like to Change?

It's come to the end of the month and you're combing through your check book and trying to figure out how you're going to pay that one bill. You're tired of being frustrated when faced with this dilemma each month. Is there any way that you can just be able to pay for everything and have some money left over?

Many of us deal with this situation. It feels like the bills pile up and that there is always that one or two that you don't have enough money to pay. It's frustrating and we would give anything to be able to have some extra money to enjoy ourselves with.

What if I told you that there was a way to make that happen? I'm not suggesting a drastic career change or anything like that. However, by changing the way we view and spend money can help us make our hard earned money go further each month. If you doubt what I'm saying, I challenge you to try to implement some of these habits into your life and see if they will work for you.

Money is a stressful and frustrating element for many. It always feels as though you work and never have anything to show for it. Some take this as the way it has to be, while others want to find ways to change this reality. By reading this book, you are saying that you want to change this and make it possible to have more at the end of the month. You want to find ways to change in order to make this happen.

If you're ready to change your financial habits in order to build financial stability and freedom, then read further. You alone have to be willing to make changes and work them into your life. Take that lead and make some changes!

Chapter 2- How to Build Healthy and Lasting Habits

Habits are difficult to build, and even more difficult to get rid of when necessary. A habit takes about thirty days to create. This means that you do the same thing for that thirty days until it becomes natural to you. Building habits takes motivation and follow through. If you want to build habits, then you must be prepared to put a lot of hard work and effort into making it happen.

The concept of habit stacking makes building habits easier and more manageable. If you take on too many habits at once, then you're setting yourself up for failure. So, it is recommended that you start with the most necessary habits and build upon them in order to make long lasting and effective habits.

Recognizing Areas that need to be Changed

In order to identify habits that you would like to break or build, you really need to know what areas of your life need to be changed. In this book, we are focusing on financial habits, but a habit can be anything that you do on a regular basis that can affect your life. Take some time and list some of the habits that are affecting your life. These can be good or bad. If you find some habits that you would like to implement, highlight those and find ways to make them a part of your life.

However, you cannot change your entire existence at once. Not only is this impossible, but you're putting way too much stress on yourself. With that much stress, you will go back to your old ways, ultimately failing at your initial intentions. Take change in small doses. This can be done by using a method called habit stacking.

Habit Stacking

So, what is habit stacking? Well, it's a concept used by some to build new habits upon existing ones. For example, you want to lose weight. The first habit that you decide to build is going to be modifying your diet so that it is healthier. After you have a good eating habit, then you want to build upon that habit with exercise. Maybe after that, you chose to join a gym. These are all habits, but habits that have been added to each other gradually. If you were to take them all on at once, you might be overwhelmed and give up before you even get a chance to begin.

Building a habit starts with basic components. First of all, you want to identify the habit and where you want it to take you. Once you have identified the habit that you want to build, then you want to decide what the end result will look like. Secondly, you will want to think of the steps that you will need to take in order to develop this habit into your personal life. These steps might be different for you than for anyone else. It's great to take suggestions, but know that you are different from others and have to make the steps reflect your needs.

After you have identified the habits and the steps that you need to take to reach the final outcome, it's time to set goals to make the habit a reality. Setting goals is a great way to put time limits on outcomes and track your progress towards the end goal. However, setting obtainable goals can be difficult within itself.

Setting a Good Goal

When you set a goal, you want to make sure that it is challenging, but you are still able to reach it. Setting a goal that is too difficult to obtain will only discourage you and make you give up on what you want to accomplish. So, take a good look at what you want to achieve and set a goal that is obtainable. Once you have a goal that meets this criteria, give yourself a time period after which you will check in and monitor your progress.

Once you have accomplished your goal, make a new goal that will challenge you again. The thing about goals is that you need to be able to accomplish them and move on to new goals. Don't set yourself back by achieving and goal and settling for it.

Now that you have a good idea of what habit stacking and goal setting entails, let's look at some habits you can begin building in order to obtain financial freedom and overall happiness.

Chapter 3- New Habits for Saving Money

It might be difficult for you to save money if you feel like all of your income goes to paying bills and other necessities. When shopping, you look with disdain at the women who are juggling their coupons at the checkout. Saving money is a concept that you can only dream about. However, it can be a true possibility. Let's take a look at some ways you can save money and be able to establish a savings account.

Clipping Coupons

I get it. You don't want to be the annoying coupon lady at the checkout stand. You know the one. Watching the screen to make sure the coupon processes correctly and arguing with the cashier when it doesn't. Meanwhile, a line a mile long builds up behind her.

I'm not suggesting that you dumpster dive for coupons and watch the minute details of the transaction. However, coupons do have great benefits. If you find a coupon for an item that you are going to purchase anyway, why not use it? It can save you a lot of money in the long run. The great part of coupons is that they're becoming electronic, so you don't have to spend hours searching and clipping them. You just check the ones you want to use.

Be careful with coupons though. I find that I will actually spend more if I find a coupon I want to use. Only use a coupon if you're planning on purchasing the item in the first place.

Go on Sale Days

Sale days can be one of the most crowded and frustrating days to visit a retail establishment. People are elbowing and fighting for the items on the shelves. However, if shopped right, sale days can yield great savings. If you're grocery shopping, sales tend to span a time frame, so you can visit the store when it's most convenient for you. Stores have sale ads that come out on a regular basis, so by knowing where the items you are shopping for are on sale, you're setting yourself up for more savings.

Look for Gas Stations with Lower Prices

I find it amazing that I can drive less than a mile and find gas prices that vary about twenty cents per gallon. If I would have waited a few more minutes, I could have saved more money. You can. There are apps for your smartphone that will list the gas prices of local gas stations. By going to one that has a lower per gallon price, the cents will add up to a great amount of savings over time.

Make Your Own Cleaners

Household cleaners are a fast way to spend a lot of money in one shopping trip. There is one for everything! However, homemade cleaners and detergents can accomplish the same goals as what you see on the shelf. Sure, they take time to make, but if you have them ready for use, you can save a ton of money by not buying a specialized product at the store.

Don't Buy it Unless It's on Sale

If you have an item that you can live without and you find that it's not on sale where you're shopping, don't buy it until it is on sale or you have a coupon. Sometimes you cannot avoid paying full price for products, but if you can, try to avoid buying it until it is on sale. By doing this, you can save money over time.

Be Able to Negotiate

There are places that you can negotiate for a better price on items. The car dealership being one. Don't be afraid to negotiate for a better price. The salesperson is trying to get as much money out of you as possible, and that can make it intimidating and difficult to shave money off of the price. However, you're trying to save money, so you have an agenda too. Don't be afraid to speak up.

Set Up a Savings Account

Saving money can be difficult, especially when you don't have money to save. What I like to do is budget a small amount of money per month to put into a savings account that I do not use unless it's an emergency. Having these funds ready and available can ease stress when you don't have enough money for what needs to be paid.

Put Your Change in a Jar

I've gotten to the point where I pay for everything using cash. By only having a certain amount of cash available for certain aspects of my finances. When that money is gone, that means that I go without until the next payday. Using cash, there is always change involved. So, whenever I have change, I make it a habit to throw it into a bucket that I cash in every so often. This is a great way to save fun money and not have it affect my finances!

Budget Your Income

One key to managing your finances is knowing where you spend your money. This can take some time, but sit down and figure out where your money goes. What bills do you need to pay and how much are they? How much money is going towards nonsense? By knowing where your money is going, you will be better able to adjust what you're spending money on and being able to save money that you're essentially throwing away.

Buy Only What is Needed

It's hard when you see good sales while walking through a store. However, take a moment and ask yourself if you really need that item. I find that most of the great sales I find end up pushed to the back of the cupboard and end up being wasted money. So, the next time you're looking at a great sale, take a moment and really ask yourself whether or not you would actually use it or whether it just looks great right now.

Repurposing Old Items

If you have old items around the house that can be used for different purposes, then convert them! Some items we have no use for in their intended capacity, but if you're creative, you can make an item function in many different ways. Not only will this keep your home from being cluttered with items that you cannot use, but it will also save you money because you don't have to find an item for that purpose!

Pick Up a Side Job

For some, this is a total impossibility. However, for others, having a small side job that earns a little extra money can help with the bills and having extra money at the end of the month. For example, you can babysit for a friend one night a week or make crafts that you can sell. A side job doesn't mean that you have to go to a job and work extra hours, but that you're doing something that can earn you extra money.

Live Where You can Afford

Again, you must focus on necessity in order live within your means. So, when you're looking at homes that are above your means, you are setting yourself up for debt. Make sure that you are finding a home where you can easily afford the monthly payments. It might not seem like your ideal, but things can change so that you can pursue that ideal in the future.

Avoid Unnecessary Spending

People are in the habit of spending money that they don't necessarily have. This can both be harmful financially and in other aspects of your life. If you don't need something, then it usually goes to waste. And if you like to hold onto things, it can easily become clutter in your home. So, make sure that you need the item before you put your money into it.

Make a List, Stick to it

When you're going shopping for groceries, make a list and stick to it closely. This can take time and be frustrating at first, but if you're only buying what you need, then you're not buying in excess. Pretty soon, you will be able to see that you're saving money by not buying items impulsively.

Telling yourself "no" can be difficult at times, especially if you like to be able to go out and buy whatever you want whenever you want. Don't limit yourself, but don't spoil yourself either. Make sure that you have a good balance between what you're earning and what you're spending.

Chapter 4- New Habits for Reducing Your Debt

Debt is a common block to financial freedom. We live in a time and a country where everyone likes to live beyond their means. Credit card companies feed on this. You find yourself with a mortgage for a home that you really cannot afford. You borrow money from friends and family in order to pay bills. There are many types of debt that one can fall into. How you deal with your debt will make a difference in getting rid of it or drowning in in.

Pay More than the Minimum Payment

If you're able to do it, pay more on a bill than you are billed. This is especially true for credit cards where the minimum payment often covers only a small portion of the entire bill. If you pay just the minimum, then the interest keeps building up so that you're spending much more than you originally planned on. Put a little more than the minimum payment toward the bill and you will avoid a lot of this interest.

Cut Up Your Credit Cards

This might be difficult for you, but credit cards are a huge source of debt. By cutting up all but one credit card, you are saying that you are planning on paying them off and never using them again. I suggest keeping one card on hand for emergencies and showing that you are using credit. However, multiple credit cards can easily lead you to financial ruin.

Focus on One Debt at a Time

Take some time and list all of your debts. If they include credit cards, note the percentage that you pay in interest. If you have high interest credit cards, focus on paying those off first. Getting rid of the cards with the highest interest rates will save you more money. While you focus on paying the higher interest credit cards off first, be sure that you're at least making minimum payments on the other bills. Late fees and accruing interest can add up to big trouble.

Pay Attention to Due Dates

Credit card companies love to hit you up with late fees. Even if your bill shows no late fee, you will find that having late payments can be harmful to your credit. So, if you're looking to buy a home or a vehicle, late payments can be a huge roadblock to this happening. Keep track of when the bill is due and make every effort to have it mailed out or paid electronically before the due date. A lot of companies offer automatic payments, so if you can keep track of what's coming out of your bank account, this might be a convenient route to ensure timely payment.

Limit the Number of Debts You Have

If you're already in debt, you might be laughing at this one. However, if you think about it, you were the one who got yourself into debt. If you hadn't purchased such and such on that credit card, then you wouldn't have had the debt. So, when another opportunity to accrue debt comes along, think hard and long before jumping into it. Some debts are unavoidable, such as medical bills and home repairs. Know the difference between a choice debt and a necessary debt.

Live Within Your Means

If you have a job at a fast food restaurant, chances are that you won't have the means to buy a home or a new car. Taking out loans will only put your further into debt. So, when considering what you need to purchase and what you want to purchase, look at the numbers. If you didn't have a loan, would you actually be able to pay for it? If the answer is "no," then you are not living within your means.

Learn to Say No to New Debt

I talked a little about this above. When a new offer for a credit card or store credit card seems to be knocking at your door, know when to say no. Credit card companies love your business because they make bank on the interest. Too many credit cards just spells trouble. If you want to pursue financial freedom, get rid of as many credit products as you can.

Avoid Binge Shopping

I know that when I get depressed, I love to go shopping. When I see something I like, I buy it. It's only later that I regret this decision. I look at my bank account and realize I really didn't have the money for that type of shopping. That's when I either eat the cost or return the items. Returning unplanned buys is embarrassing for me, so I tend to take the financial hit instead. So, if you have a spending habit like mine, try and find ways that you can relieve your mood without visiting a retail establishment!

Budget High

When I put together my budget, I always budget more than the actual bill. By having this cushion, if something should come up and I do have to pay more, than I'm prepared for it. This also helps me to make sure that I have enough to cover everything for the month.

Give Up Things

If you don't need it, then give it up. Being frugal isn't all about money, but what you have in other possessions as well. Having too much can make your life complicated and cluttered. Learn to shed some things to live happily and frugally.

Avoid Credit

As mentioned before, credit has an ugly way of sucking up your finances. By avoiding getting involved in credit, you're not overpaying for the items you buy. I have two store credit cards that I use to keep my credit high just in case I need to use it, but for the most part, if I don't have money to buy it, I don't.

Learning ways to reduce your debt will help you to see more money at the end of the month. If you don't have the money, don't spend it! That is why most people tend to be in debt. They spend money they don't have. By only getting what you need and not using credit to get there, you're on your way to being frugal and seeing a positive end result.

Chapter 5- New Habits for Changing the Way You Spend Money

It might be a difficult concept to change how you spend your money. After all, you earned it, so aren't you entitled to spend it how you would like? Yes and no. While you do earn your money, you have to be wise on how you use it. Spending money on silly items will be a waste. However, you see people doing this all the time. They like it, so they buy it. This ends up giving you a lot of clutter and not enough money. So, by changing how you view and spend your money, you will be well on your way to finding financial freedom.

Think Twice Before Purchasing

It may seem awkward for a while, but when you're considering buying something that may not be necessary, take a step back and think through the scenarios. Will it be used? Is it useful to your life? Can you do without it? After answering a set of questions, then you will be able to make an informed decision about the prospective purchase.

Put Items Back

If you like to throw things into the cart as you go, learn to look through your cart and put at least a third of your cart back. If you have a list and sticking to that list, then you won't have to worry about this step. However, if you're just going on the fly, then you probably have too much in your cart.

Buy Only What You Need

When shopping, make a list and stick to it. That way, you're only buying what you need and not anything extra. If the temptation rises to buy extra, keep walking.

Treat Yourself Every Once in a While

Being frugal doesn't mean doing without. So, when you feel like you need a little pick-me-up, treat yourself to something that you enjoy. Don't totally deny yourself simply to save money all the time.

Use Cash Instead of Cards

I found that if I budget with cash, it's easier for me to not spend extra. At the beginning of the month, I will set aside enough money for gas, groceries, and any other thing that I need. Once that money is spent, it's gone and I have to wait until the next budget to buy more. However, if it's a situation of starving, I will bend that rule, but for the most part, it cuts down on excess spending when shopping.

Use a Handbasket for Small Trips

When you know that you only need a few items, grab a handbasket instead of a full cart. This will limit your temptation to throw items that you don't need into the cart. I found that I have saved myself a lot of money because I don't stock up on unnecessary items.

Weigh the Pros and Cons of the Purchase

If it's a sizeable purchase, think through it before you buy it. A candy bar is one thing while an entire patio set is another. Look at the entire picture of the purchase. How will it be used and how will it affect your finances? By thinking through the purchase, you're making it an informed decision rather than a spontaneous purchase.

Know What Your Bank Accounts Look Like at All Times

If you use a debit card, know what you're spending and how much is in your account at all times. Banks are making this easier by having mobile apps that will tell you how much you have at all times. If you don't know what you have, you run the risk of overspending and accruing bank fees that will cost you even more.

Know When to Walk Away

If you know that something isn't necessary and that you cannot afford it, learn to step away from it and save it for another day. Odds are that you're going to forget that you wanted it in the first place and not even miss it.

Avoid Spontaneous Shopping Trips

Make sure that you're planning your shopping trips. This means making a list and knowing approximately what you plan to spend at that particular place. This will give you a guideline as to what you need as opposed to impulse buying.

By knowing and changing you spending habits, you will find that your spending abilities are actually greater. You have control of what you spend and what you buy rather than an impulse that you regret later. Take a good look at your spending habits and see what areas you can change in order to ensure that you're not spending money unnecessarily.

Chapter 6- Learning to Only Buy What is Needed

In our society, we value having as much as we possibly can. However, this can damage both our self-esteem and our pocketbooks if we're not careful. Look around you. How much of what you see is an absolute necessity? Not very much, I'm guessing. While it's nice to have nice belongings, it can also cause you financial hardships trying to get to the point where you feel like you can compare to others.

Learning to say no to some of the things that you feel you should have takes time and discipline. It's not impossible, though. You just need to get into the habit of seeing what you need before you purchase it. In this chapter, I'm going to give you some ideas of how to evaluate whether or not you need something rather than simply wanting it.

Stop Before You Buy

When you're considering buying a certain item, stop for a moment and evaluate the whole picture. What are you going to use it for? Is there another way to avoid having to buy the new item? Is it priced too highly? Could you wait for a sale? Really take all of the options into perspective and make an informed decision on your purchases.

Evaluate Whether You Need the Item

You're at the store and about to buy something that has caught your attention. However, you know that you really don't need it and that it won't get much use. Would you be willing to live without it? Is it necessary for your life? Know what you're getting into before buying something that will sit unused and end up being a waste of money.

Putting Things Back

We mentioned this in a prior chapter. While shopping, if you know that the purchase is sheer impulse, put it back. You would rather do this while you're in the store rather than when you're at home and are forced to return the item. It's much easier to say no before purchasing than going back to the store to return an item!

Wish List vs. Need List

I have started a new system in my household. When there is something that catches our eyes, we have two lists that the item can be put on. The need list includes items that will be necessary and useful for the person. The wish list is the list that includes what the person would like to have but they really don't need.

Know What is Needed Before Going into a Store

There are many different ways to ensure that you're buying only what is needed when you go to a store. I have mentioned lists in the previous chapters, but there are also methods to keep family members from putting things that are not needed into the cart. In my household, we have an understanding that we go by the list and need to talk about anything that seems to jump out at us when we are actually at the store. That way, financial frugality is the responsibility of the entire family, not just the adults.

Another thing I like to do is give the kids an allowance. This is money that they can spend as they feel necessary. When that money is gone, then it's gone until they receive the next allowance. I believe that this teaches them financial responsibility and how to save and spend their money.

It is incredibly important that you understand necessary purchases as opposed to unnecessary purchases. With so many different messages about what you need or want, it can get difficult to know what is needed as opposed to a luxury. If you have trouble telling the difference between the two, then think back to your basic needs. Think food, shelter, and security and know what gets those for you. If you don't find that it's necessary to meet your basic needs, then it becomes a wish rather than a need.

Know what you need and buy accordingly. It's okay to treat yourself every once in a while, but you must make sure that you're not overdoing it on a regular basis. Being frugal isn't about self-denial, but about learning self-control.

Chapter 7- Enjoying a Stress-free and Happy Financial Life

Once you understand financial freedom and living frugally, you will find that it is still an enjoyable way to live. Just because you don't have what everyone thinks you should have to be happy doesn't mean that you cannot be happy. Once I cut down on buying unnecessary garbage, I found that I was able to pay my bills more easily and not have to worry about coming up short at the end of the month. Having that financial assurance took away a large amount of stress in my life.

Worrying about your finances is one of the most stressful things in life. Emergencies happen, we tend to not think through purchases, and then we find ourselves dipping into our savings accounts or borrowing money from relatives or friends in order to meet our basic needs. If we had only thought through the financial situation earlier, we might have avoided the entire situation.

Being wise with your money is just one way that you can make a huge impact on your financial freedom. Many of us have debt. However, if we focus on eliminating debt and living within our means, then we can enjoy a happier lifestyle. If you find that you're in a job where you're not making enough to support even a simple lifestyle, consider changing jobs if possible. Your ambitions and self-control are just a few of the factors that can make it a worthwhile change.

I'm not telling you that this is going to be easy. For some it will be easier for than others. However, there are many bad spending habits that people have that can be difficult to change. Take your financial habits one habit at a time. Don't overwhelm yourself by trying to make multiple changes at once. Habit stacking is a great concept that promotes change without being overwhelmed by it.

Have goals, but don't set your ambitions too high to begin with. In order to build long and lasting habits, you must take changes in small steps. It is easy to give up on something because it's too hard. This is what happens when we try to take on too much at once. Just remember that by taking one habit at a time that you're setting yourself up for long lasting change rather than utter failure.

After building some healthy frugal financial goals in my home, I find that the stress levels have gone down, making everyone much happier. Everyone has a part in making sure that the spending is going in the right direction. Not only are we building healthy financial habits as a family, but we are teaching our children the responsibilities of money.

If you're ready to make some changes so that you are living a more frugal life, I encourage you to choose some healthy habits to pursue and begin to work on them. It can only help you to be more liberated financially and reduce the stress of living paycheck to paycheck.

Good luck on your pursuit of a healthy and frugal financial life!

Conclusion

Thank you again for downloading this book!

I hope this book was able to help you to find good financial habits to build in order to obtain frugality in your personal life. Financial stresses are one of the main problems that prevent people from being happy. However, it doesn't have to be that way. With a few changes to your mindset and your habits, you can be well on your way to financial freedom.

The next step is to identify the areas in your life where you need to change your spending habits. Try using some of the ideas in this book to help you change your habits and your mindset about money. Once you can build positive financial habits, you will be well on your way to overcoming debt and living a happier and more frugal lifestyle!

Finally, if you enjoyed this book, then I'd like to ask you for a favor, would you be kind enough to leave a review for this book on Amazon? It'd be greatly appreciated!

Made in the USA
Coppell, TX
12 October 2020

39678899R10111